THE HISTORY
OF HISTORICAL WRITING
IN AMERICA

BY

J. FRANKLIN JAMESON, Ph. D.

PROFESSOR OF HISTORY IN BROWN UNIVERSITY

BOSTON AND NEW YORK
HOUGHTON, MIFFLIN AND COMPANY
The Riverside Press, Cambridge
1891

55539

The Riverside Press, Cambridge, Mass., U. S. A.
Printed by H. O. Houghton & Company.

PREFACE

THESE four Lectures upon the history of historical writing in America were read before public audiences in the hall of the Johns Hopkins University in January and February, 1887, and in that of Brown University in February and March, 1889. The third and fourth were printed in *Englische Studien* in 1888 and 1889, and the four, after a considerable revision, appeared in the *New England Magazine* in 1891.

BROWN UNIVERSITY, PROVIDENCE
May 2, 1891

CONTENTS

THE HISTORY OF HISTORICAL WRITING IN AMERICA.

————

I.

THE HISTORIANS OF THE SEVENTEENTH CENTURY.

THE history of historical writing in the English colonies and in the United States falls, naturally, into four periods; and this alike whether we take as the basis of our classification its characteristics as historical literature, or its characteristics as historical science. In the first period, the heroic age of discovery and settlement, such history as we have is the work of the Argonauts themselves, who, with little consciousness of authorship, still less of membership in a literary profession, wrote down, in simplicity of mind, accounts of things which they had seen and in which they had themselves borne a great part. This period is roughly

equivalent to the seventeenth century. Upon
this followed two or three generations of
what we might call epigonal historiography,
bearing clear marks of a colonial or provin-
cial origin, yet often careful and scholarly,
and mainly devoted to investigating and re-
cording with pious care the achievements of
those who had preceded. The third period,
lasting from the Revolution to the Civil
War, was one in which history shared, in
common with other departments, the effects
of the general effort toward the creation of
an independent American literature. During this, the classical period of our historical writing, the favorite subjects were portions of European history. Since then we
have had a marked improvement in method
and scholarship; but the dominant impulse
of the fourth period has been toward a
closer, and especially a broader, study of
our own history. It is with these four periods that the chapters of this book are respectively to be occupied. In general, only
the most important writers of each will be
considered; and no effort will be made to
relate at length the picturesque and interesting details of these writers' lives, — not
from any such disdain of the picturesque as

modern students of history are supposed to
affect, but because the subject is not the
lives and personalities of American historians, but the development of American historiography.

In the time of the first adventurers and
settlers, some historical literature of value
had already been produced by the nation
from which they sprang, — chronicles like
those of Hall and Holinshed, collections
like those of Stow, and a few more notable
performances, Lord Bacon's " Henry VII.,"
Knollys' " Historie of the Turkes," Fox's
" Martyrs," and the great fragment of a
" History of the World " which Raleigh
had composed during his long imprisonment
in the Tower. But no one of these was in
any way the model of our earliest historians,
whose purposes were quite different. The
purpose of one class was to awaken immediate interest in a given colony, and stimulate
immigration into it by accounts of what had
been done there; to this class belong Captain John Smith and Captain Edward Johnson. The model of some of them may be
seen in the pages of Hakluyt, in the Relations and Narratives of voyagers. The
other class, of which Governor Bradford and

Governor Winthrop are the chief exam-
ples, believing themselves to have been concerned in memorable beginnings, wrote for
the benefit of posterity permanent memorials,
which they did not intend to be published
till after their deaths. It is to these four,
as best deserving, among our writers of the
seventeenth century, the name of historian,
that the present chapter is to be mainly
given.

At the beginning at once of our colonial history and of American historical literature stands the burly figure of Captain
John Smith; and yet he stands somewhat
apart from both. There is no need to re-
count at length the stirring events of his
early life, — how, after wandering over
much of Europe and the Levant, he took
service against the Turk, slew three Turk-
ish cavaliers in single combat before the
walls of Regall, was captured and sold as
a slave, was befriended by a noble lady at
Constantinople, was sent to serve as a slave
in Crim-Tartary, and escaped with many
adventures; but it is plain, from the nature
of them, that he belonged in character to
the generation that had just passed away.
He had more in common with Hawkins and

Frobisher and Drake, with those who re-
pulsed the Armada, and sought Eldorado,
and braved the northern ice, and " singed
the King of Spain's beard," with all the
freshness and buoyancy and adventurous-
ness of the Elizabethans, than with Eliot
and Pym and Selden, with the sobriety, the
seriousness, the prosaic strenuousness, which
had begun to overspread and to characterize
the England of James I. It was these traits
of character that made him really unsuited
to much of the work which now needed to
be done in the American settlements. He
was a colonial adventurer in a generation
of colonial founders. At the beginning, the
services of such a man were invaluable, and
the colony probably owed more to him than
to any other man during the thirty months
that he spent in it. But, the initial work
once done, another sort of talent was needed
if the colony was to be, not abortive, as the
Elizabethan colonial experiments had been,
but a strong and prosperous community,
founded on sober and humdrum agriculture
and trade; and so the shrewd London merchants of the Virginia Company were not
wrong in making no further use of Smith.

The same qualities shine conspicuous in

the writings of Smith, and mark him off
from the rest as, though the precursor, yet
not the father of the American historical
writers.   His writings breathe the spirit
that invests the pages of Hakluyt and Pur-
chas with so surpassing and so imperishable
a charm, not that which has made our colonial history dull and our nation great.   He
writes, by preference, of encounters, of ex-
plorations, of opportunities for present gain,
as one who is directing a band of adventurers, not as one who is thoughtfully laying
foundations for the gradual growth of a
mighty state.   He does not lack seriousness, but he is more a knight-errant than a
man of business.   But if both his rôle and
his attitude are those of a knight-errant,
bearing in his veins the enthusiastic blood
of the sixteenth century, but set to do the
sober tasks of the seventeenth, he was in
the main a worthy knight, fearing God after the simple, untroubled fashion of the
earlier time, without overmuch sojourning
in Meshec and Kedar, serving faithfully and
energetically his king and the company, giving good government, and doing with his
might what his hand found to do.   He
wrote of all this with keen zest and enjoy-

ment, and with not too much of modesty, or of mildness toward his adversaries; but when was a knight-errant ever modest or conciliatory?

The strictly historical works of Captain John Smith are but two in number. The first is a brief tract of thirty or forty pages, entitled "A True Relation of such occurrences and accidents of noate as hath happened in Virginia since the first planting of that Collony, which is now resident in the South part thereof, till the last returne from thence." The second is the extensive book entitled "The Generall Historie of Virginia, New-England, and the Summer Isles," a brief continuation of which was printed as part second of his "True Travels, Adventures, and Observations." His other books are mostly of a descriptive character: they have a value as historical material; they are not themselves historical writings. The "True Relation" was written in Virginia about the end of May, 1608, when the colony had been in existence a little more than a year; it was sent home by Captain Nelson in the Phœnix, and was published at London in August. It is only a pamphlet, and a somewhat hastily prepared one at that. It is mainly occupied with the personal adventures of Smith himself, the exploring expeditions which he conducted, and his dealings with the Indians. Not much is told us of events at Jamestown. While that little is valuable, in the paucity of eye-witness accounts of the first year's doings, its value is much diminished, or at least rendered doubtful, by the fact that it is everywhere seen to be colored by Smith's hostility to certain fellow-members of the Council. Which was right in their frequent quarrels is hard now to determine ; but no one can fail to see that Smith was too censorious of the actions of others, too vain of his own, to be a historical witness of the highest degree of merit.

The same animosities are to be found, unallayed after a period of sixteen years, in the " Generall Historie," published in 1620, the book which forms Smith's chief title to be numbered among the American historians. Or rather, it exhibits these animosities widened into partisanship in a more important conflict, and applied to the events of a greater number of years. Coming home in 1609, and never afterward succeeding in getting employment from the

company, Smith seems to have extended his
resentment againt those who had ruled the
colony with him to their successors, and
eventually to the managers of the company.
In the last years of James I., the Virginia
Company's proceedings reflected the conflict
going on in the country at large, the minor-
ity being of the court party, the managers
belonging to the opposition. Smith takes
many opportunities in the "Generall Historie" to attack them, to accuse the mis-
management of the colony since he left it,
and to lament that his advice was not rather
followed and his services employed. "I
know," he adds, "I shall be taxed for writing so much of my selfe; but I care not
much, because the judiciall know there are
few such Souldiers as [those who] have
writ their owne actions, nor know I who
will or can tell my intents better then my
selfe."

The book which the doughty captain had
prepared with so resolute a disregard of all
natural impulses toward self-effacement was
proposed, as the records of the Virginia
Company show, as early as 1621, but published in 1624, in a volume of two hundred
and fifty pages folio, embellished with sev-

eral quaint and well-engraved maps. Smith
was, after all, the author of only about
seventy-five pages out of the two hundred
and fifty; and of these seventy-five, nearly
seventy comprise mere reprints from three
of his descriptive books. Of all the rest
he was but the editor or compiler. The
composition of the book is in fact singular.
The first book, treating of the English voyages to Virginia before 1607, is entirely a
compilation or patchwork of previous narratives. The second book is a reprinted description of Virginia as it was in 1607.
The third book is a republication, with some
variations, of a body of narratives by some
of the original planters, which had been
edited by one Dr. Simonds, and published
in 1612; they cover the thirty months of
Smith's stay in the colony, and are from
persons belonging to his faction. What he
himself has contributed to this division is
limited to the insertion, here and there, of
verses more remarkable for sententiousness
than for beauty, and, it must be added, the
addition of striking adventures not mentioned in the " True Relation," and a general heightening of the picturesqueness of
his own career. The fourth book, giving

the history of Virginia from 1609 to 1624, is almost wholly a compilation, or rather a transcription, of the narratives of residents; the fifth, treating of the history of the Bermudas, is wholly so. Finally, to make Book VI., entitled "The Generall Historie of New England," he reprints his "Description of New England," 1616, and "New England's Trials," 1620, inserts Edward Winslow's "Plantation in New England," and, with a few interesting pages on the present estate of New Plymouth, closes this remarkable historical mosaic, of which it may almost be said that what is historical is not his, and what is his is not historical. But herein, also, we must confess, he has been the precursor of many of our historical writers, not all of whom have enumerated as frankly as he the victims of their scissors.

Nothing has been said, thus far, of the story of the saving of Smith by Pocahontas. The historical student who is not entirely steeped in haughty professionalism, who would himself "strictly meditate the thankless Muse," yet wishes to temper that austere cult with a regard for the unscientific preferences of Amaryllis and Neæra, will cer-

tainly hesitate long before assailing the most
famous of the few romantic legends of our
early colonial history. And yet it appears
that, in spite of a dozen novels and perhaps
a gross of poems that have gathered about
it, the legend must go. A whole chapter
would hardly be long enough for a full dis-
cussion of the arguments, but in brief the
case is this. Not only is there no mention
of such an episode in the full account of his
Chickahominy expedition which Smith gave,
a few months after he went upon it, in the
"True Relation," but everything there indicates a most friendly reception by Pow-
hatan; nor do any of his companions mention an adventure so striking. It first appears in print in the "Generall Historie"
of 1624, interpolated as one of those em-
bellishments of his friends' accounts, to
which allusion has been made. It appears
that Smith, in 1616, hinted at such a service performed by Pocahontas, in a letter to
the Queen, written when Pocahontas was in
England. In short, the probability is that
he invented the episode in order to connect
himself in a picturesque manner with one
who had lately been attracting so much attention. One need not stop to defend his-

torical criticism for destroying so pretty a legend, for historical criticism brings to light two stories of heroism that are true where it removes one that is false; but perhaps we may more easily be reconciled to the loss of this particular romance if we remember that, pictures and poems and story-books to the contrary notwithstanding, the real Pocahontas was only ten years old at the time of the alleged rescue.

To turn from Captain John Smith to Governor William Bradford is like turning from "Amadis of Gaul" to the "Pilgrim's Progress." The worthy governor of Plymouth Plantation had slain no Turks, had undergone no romantic adventures, had been signally befriended by no princesses or noble dames, whether heathen, Mohammedan, or Christian. But if fortune denied him interesting adventures, — except in so far as the high purposes of the Pilgrim Fathers and the permanent importance of their work invest all that they did with interest, — it did not deal so with his book. The story of its vicissitudes is a curious one. It was well known to historical scholars that Governor Bradford had left behind him a manuscript history of Plymouth Plantation.

Some extracts from it had been given in
print by certain historical writers of the
hundred years succeeding his death, the last
being Governor Hutchinson, in 1767. It
was supposed that Bradford's descendants
had lent it to the Rev. Thomas Prince, the
noted historical scholar of Boston, and that
Prince had deposited it in the New England Library which he was forming, in the
tower of the Old South Church. During
the first year of the Revolutionary War,
while Boston was occupied by the British,
that church was, as is well known, used by
them as a riding-school. After that time,
nothing was heard of the precious manuscript of Bradford's history, until, one day
in 1855, a local antiquary most unexpectedly
found a trace of it. While reading a small
English book by Bishop Wilberforce on the
history of the Protestant Episcopal Church
in America, he came upon certain passages
which were identical with some of the extracts from Bradford given, as already mentioned, by American writers of the last
century. The foot-notes of the book described these passages as taken from a manuscript history of the Plantation of Plymouth,
in the library of the Bishop of London at

Fulham. The discovery was communicated to one of the leading members of the Massachusetts Historical Society, and a correspondence was entered upon. The manuscript in the bishop's library was proved to be that of Governor Bradford's long-lost history, and was copied, and printed in 1856. How it came to be in the Fulham library no one knows; nor does any one know how to get it back from there.

However, we have the printed text, and a most important and interesting work it is. Governor Bradford's qualifications for preparing such a history are manifest. From the first year of the settlement down to the time of his death — during a period, that is, of thirty-six years — there had been but five years in which he had not been elected governor of the colony. He had been among the earlier fugitives to Holland, and was, therefore, personally cognizant of the history of the little community in the period preceding its transfer to America. During most of the long period of his governorship he had had in mind the preparation of such an account, of which it appears that he wrote the beginning in 1630, and the end in 1650, and had been saving and collecting letters

and documents important to his purpose.
He had, therefore, the most entire familiarity with the history of the colony, and
time enough to insure deliberation and
care. Moreover, he had not only a thoughtful mind and a high degree of intelligence,
but was even, like so many of the early
American governors, a man of some scholarship. Cotton Mather says of him : " He
was a person for study as well as action;
and hence, notwithstanding the difficulties
through which he passed in his youth, he
attained unto a notable skill in languages ;
the Dutch tongue was become almost as
vernacular to him as the English; the
French tongue he could also manage ; the
Latin and the Greek he had mastered; but
the Hebrew he most of all studied, because,
he said, he would see with his own eyes
the ancient oracles of God in their native
beauty. He was also well skilled in history,
in antiquity, and in philosophy; and for
theology, he became so versed in it that he
was an irrefragable disputant against . . .
errors. . . . But the crown of all was his
holy, prayerful, watchful, and fruitful walk
with God, wherein he was very exemplary."
It may illustrate the cast of Bradford's mind

to repeat what he himself has said in regard
to one of these studies. Eight manuscript
pages of Hebrew roots with English equiva-
lents, and of Hebrew exercises, have been
found, written in his handwriting, and pre-
faced with these remarks : " Though I am
growne aged, yet I have had a longing desire to see, with my owne eyes, something
of that most ancient language, and holy
tongue, in which the law and oracles of God
were writ; and in which God and angels
spake to the holy patriarchs of old time ; and
what names were given to things, from the
creation. And though I cannot attaine to
much herein, yet I am refreshed to have
seen some glimpse hereof (as Moyses saw
the land of Canan afarr of). My aim and
desire is, to see how the words and phrases
lye in the holy texte ; and to discerne somewhat of the same, for my owne contente."

But whatever scholarship the excellent
governor may have had, he does not obtrude
it into his book, which has nothing of the
pedantic manner so frequent in the seventeenth century. He writes a plain, sober,
and straightforward account, the evident
care and accuracy of which make it one of
the most valued sources for our colonial

1*

period. His narrative covers the history of
the colony down to the year 1646, at which
point it was left unfinished. It embraces
the events which led, in England and Holland, to the exodus of the Pilgrims, the now
familiar tale of their early sufferings and
achievements, the occasional controversies in
which they were involved, their negotiations
with other colonies, their troubles with the
London merchants, and their correspondence
and relations with the body whom they had
left behind at their departure. The phrases
in which that departure is described are
memorable : " So they lefte that goodly and
pleasante citie, which had been ther resting
place near twelve years ; but they knew
they were pilgrimes, and looked not much
on those things, but lift up their eyes to the
heavens, their dearest countrie, and quieted
their spirits." Such words as these, which
have been often quoted, do not stand alone
in the narrative ; with all its sobriety, it is
clothed in many passages with that exquisite
and singular beauty of expression which a
close familiarity with the English translation
of the Bible has so often bestowed on writers
of little literary art. Of such is the following, written in appreciative commemoration
of his companions' fortitude.

"But hear," he says, "I cannot but stay and make a pause, and stand half amased at this poore peoples presente condition; and so I thinke will the reader, too, when he well considers the same. Being thus past the vast ocean, and a sea of troubles before in their preparation, . . . they had now no friends to welcome them nor inns to entertaine or refresh their weatherbeaten bodys, no houses or much less townes to repair too, to seeke for succoure. It is recorded in scripture as a mercie to the apostle & his shipwraked company, that the barbarians shewed them no smale kindnes in refreshing them, but these savage barbarians, when they mette with them, . . . were readier to fill their sids full of arrows then otherwise. And for the season it was winter, and they that know the winters of that cuntrie know them to be sharp and violent, and subjecte to cruell and feirce stormes, deangerous to travill to known places, much more to serci an unknown coast. Besids, what could they see but a hidious and desolate wildernes, full of wild beasts and willd men? And what multituds ther might be of them they knew not. Nether could they, as it were, goe up to the tope of Pisgah, to vew from this

willdernes a more goodly cuntrie to feed
their hops; for which way soever they
turned their eys (save upward to the heavens) they could have litle solace or content
in respecte of any outward objects. . . .
Let it also be considered what weake hopes
of supply and succoure they left behind
them, that might bear up their minds in this
sade condition and trialls they were under.
. . . What could now sustaine them but the
spirite of God and his grace? May not
and ought not the children of these fathers
rightly say: Our faithers were Englishmen
which came over this great ocean, and were
ready to perish in this willdernes; but they
cried unto the Lord, and he heard their
voyce, and looked on their adversitie, &c.
Let them, therefore, praise the Lord, because
he is good, and his mercies endure forever.
Yea, let them which have been redeemed of
the Lord, shew how he hath delivered them
from the hand of the oppressour. When
they wandered in the desert willdernes out
of the way, and found no citie to dwell in,
both hungrie and thirstie, their sowle was
overwhelmed in them. Let them confess
before the Lord his loving kindnes, and his
wonderful works before the sons of men."

It is a curious good fortune by which we happen to have accounts of two of our earliest colonies, those of Plymouth and of Massachusetts Bay, written by the two men who had most to do with managing the affairs of each in the earliest period. Moreover, the two governors and historians were in some degree typical of the two colonies whose history they helped to make and to write. The Separatist colony and the Puritan colony were widely different. The history of the Pilgrim Fathers is full of suffering, of poverty, of humility, of patience, and of mildness. It is the story of a small and feeble enterprise, glorified by faith and hope and charity, but necessarily and always limited by the slender resources of the poor and humble men who originated it. The founding of the Bay colony, on the other hand, was less a colonial enterprise than a great Puritan emigration. It was organized by men of substance and standing, supported by the wealth of a great and prosperous body of the English nation, and consciously directed toward the high end of founding in America a great Puritan state. And as Massachusetts was to Plymouth Plantation, so, in many respects, was Governor John

Winthrop to Governor William Bradford.
He was, in the first place, a man of much
more prominent position, lord of the manor
of Groton, one of the attorneys of the Court
of Wards and Liveries, a magistrate, and
a man of considerable wealth. But he was
also a man of a broader, larger, and more
philosophic intellect, as well as of a more
regular and extensive education. In short,
he had more thoroughly those powers and
acquisitions of mind which would fit one
to direct worthily the larger concerns of a
strong and important state, and to describe
worthily its origin and early development.
For beauty of character, it is hard to give the
preference to either governor. Long possession of great power in a community resolute
to defend its independence and suppress
dissension with a high hand, strong, self-
reliant, and intolerant, never succeeded in
marring the exquisite sensitiveness of Winthrop's conscience, or affecting the gen-
tleness and sweetness of his deportment.
Scrupulosity of conscience we perhaps expect to find in a Puritan, but the second
point is worth a little more attention. It is
worth while frequently to insist that harshness, and sourness, and gloom were not

characteristic of all periods of Puritan history alike. Puritanism in New England, as in Old England, went through three different stages, — the period of origin and growth, the period of conflict, the period of decline. The Puritanism which was satirized in " Hudibras," and which fell with Richard Cromwell, was not the Puritanism of the civil wars. Still less was it the Puritanism of Milton's earlier years, — of " Comus " and " L'Allegro " and "Il Penseroso." In that earlier time, Puritanism had not dissevered itself from the cheerfulness and spontaneity of the Elizabethan period, but had simply added to them, on the one hand a greater degree of moral earnestness, and on the other hand a greater zeal for innovation in church and state. So it was in New England. The well-known and most amusing diary of Chief Justice Sewall shows us Puritanism as it had come to be among the men of the third generation, — Puritanism gone to seed, grown narrow and harsh and petty, and rapidly becoming mundane and Philistine. But before this, and before the preceding generation of conflict, and before the hardships of life and the wildness of nature had begun to depress

men's minds to the level of the awful right-
eousness with which we are so familiar,
there was a Puritanism of a less unlovely
type ; serious and strict, but not uncheerful,
nor insensible to the delights and beauty of
life. Of such Puritanism John Winthrop
was the type and the exponent. In him
Puritanism is seen at its best, not only car-
ing (and compelling others to care) for
what was in its opinion true and honest and
just, but also observant of whatsoever things
are lovely and of good report. The poetic
imagination which led him to prefer, of all
books of the Bible, the Song of Solomon,
the depth and beauty of his religious experi-
ences, the exquisite tenderness of his letters
to his wife, the mildness of his efficient rule
as governor, all show us a nature singularly
attractive. He was, in short, a gentleman ;
not in the spurious sense of one whose ancestors and connections have been highly
distinguished for being related to each other,
but in the better sense of one who combines
with a noble character the additional graces
of a perfect sweetness of temper and a perfect refinement of manner.

I have enlarged upon Winthrop's personal
characteristics because they were an impor-

tant factor in the composition of his book.
Of a historian of our day, writing of these
things, this need not be true. But in the
case of one who writes of the genesis of a
state of which he has been the foremost
founder, the study of his personality is a
matter of much consequence to the critic,
not only because it helps to understand his
book, but also because it helps to understand
the movement which he headed. Milton, in
a famous passage of the Apology for Smec-
tymnuus, reminds us "that he who would not
be frustrate of his hope to write well hereafter in laudable things, ought himself to be
a true poem, . . . not presuming to sing
high praises of heroic men or famous cities,
unless he have in himself the experience and
the practice of all that which is praise-
worthy." John Winthrop did have within
himself these things. They shone out plainly
in the acts of his public life, and they are not
less conspicuous in the history which he left
behind him.

The "History of New England" has the
form of annals, or even, at first, of a journal,
begun by the governor on board the Arbella
on the day when he set sail from England in
1630. It is continued to the winter of 1648,

a few months before his death. Naturally, many matters of small moment are treated in it, — minor doings of the governing body and the churches, moving accidents, remarkable providences, and so forth. But the narrative is never undignified and never gossiping. And when events of greater importance to the colony, or deliberations and discussions involving the essential principles of its policy, fall to be described, we could hardly desire a guide more impartial, more informing, or more thoughtful. Together with the actions of the rulers their reasons are set before us, and set before us with a high-minded confidence and a philosophic breadth of view that leave nothing to be desired. Once in a while occur really admirable reasonings and statements in matters of political philosophy; while the absence of passion and intolerance and pettiness is very marked. The early years of the colony were a time of strong party feeling and of bitter dissensions; yet Winthrop never takes the opportunity of private writing and posthumous publication to set down aught in malice against any of his opponents. Of the chief among them, Sir Harry Vane, he says that at all times " he showed himself a true

friend to New England, and a man of a
noble and generous mind." The severest
thing that he says of any of them, so far as
I know, is found in some words of grave
and temperate disapprobation which he uses
with regard to Governor Bellingham, and
even here he does not fail to suggest what
excuse he can for Bellingham's factious ill-
temper. Speaking in one passage of some
of these disagreements, he says: "Indeed, it
occasioned much grief to all the elders, and
gave great offence through the country; and
such as were acquainted with other states in
the world, and had not well known the persons, would have concluded such a faction
here as hath been usual in the council of
England and other states, who walk by politic principles only. But these gentlemen
were such as feared God, and endeavored to
walk by the rules of his word in all their
proceedings, so as it might be conceived in
charity that they walked according to their
judgments and conscience, and where they
went aside it was merely for want of light,
or their eyes were held through some temp-
tation for a time, that they could not make
use of the light they had; for in all these
differences and agitations about them, they

continued in brotherly love, and in the exercise of all friendly offices each to other, as
occasion required." And the story of the
governor's own reconciliation with Dudley
shows that, so far as he himself was concerned, he has not overstated the case.

Winthrop's narrative, like Bradford's, was
left in manuscript at his death, and came to
be a part of the New England Library in
the Old South Church. Its subsequent vicissitudes were curious, though not so remarkable as those of the "History of Plymouth
Plantation." After the Revolution, two of
the three volumes of the manuscript were
found in the possession of the elder branch
of the Winthrops in Connecticut, edited,
very superficially it must be said, by the re-
doubtable lexicographer, Noah Webster, and
published in 1790. In 1816, the third volume was discovered in the dormitory of the
Old South Church. The Massachusetts Historical Society entrusted the preparation of
a new edition of the whole to James Savage.
Before he had accomplished the collation of
the second volume of the manuscript, that
volume was destroyed by a fire which broke
out in his office. The first and the third
volumes are now in the library of the soci-

ety; for the second, our text is that of Webster's edition.

He who is seeking a characteristic production of the traditional Puritan should
without doubt resort to that of the fourth
and last writer upon our list. Its very title
is characteristically Puritan. It was an age
of quaint title-pages; but nowhere were they
quainter than in the books of the New England Puritans. "New England's Teares for
Old England's Feares," "New England's
Salamander Discovered," "New England's
Jonas cast up at London," "The Heart of
New England rent at the Blasphemies of
the Present Generation," and, for a longer
example, that of John Cotton's famous pamphlet, "Milk for Babes, drawn out of the
Breasts of both Testaments, chiefly for the
Spiritual Nourishment of Boston Babes, but
may be of like use to other Children," —
such are the names of some of the early historical and controversial tracts of New England. Among them all, few have a quainter
title than that which the author of the historical book before us bestowed upon it, —
"The Wonder-Working Providence of Sion's
Saviour in New England." The London
publisher saw fit to alter this upon the title-

page to "The History of New England;" but
in the head-lines of the pages the title chosen
by the author is followed throughout. A
history of New England the book is not, but
rather a history of Massachusetts down to
the year 1651. Among the New England
histories it has the distinction of having been
the first to appear in print, for it was printed
in London in 1653 (dated 1654). It was
printed anonymously, but its author is known
to have been Captain Edward Johnson, selectman and town clerk of the town of Woburn in Massachusetts. In Governor Winthrop, as 1 have declared, we may see
Puritanism at its very best. But the *élite*
of humanity are nowhere in a majority. A
better representative of the average Puritan
of the middle class is doubtless Captain
Johnson. He was a Kentish farmer, and
probably also a shipwright, who came out in
the same fleet with Winthrop in 1630. A
dozen years later, he was, in company with
half a dozen others, one of the founders of
the new town of Woburn. It is interesting
to note that, of his dozen companions in this
undertaking, one, John Sedgwick, afterward
became one of Cromwell's major-generals,
while another rose in the naval service of

England to be Rear-Admiral Thomas Graves. But the stout Kentishman, having put his hand to the plough, chose to remain in the town he had helped to plant. He had always an important part in the affairs of the town, was chosen selectman nearly every year, was again and again elected to represent the town in the general court or legislature of the colony, acted as town clerk, and was captain of the train-band. He was, therefore, more or less concerned in the public affairs in the colony, but never had a leading part in them. Though he was a more prominent, a wealthier, and perhaps a more intelligent man than most of his fellow-citizens, we may well enough take him as in most respects a type of the rank and file of the original settlers. This is in the main what gives its value to this first printed history of Massachusetts.

Captain Edward Johnson was far inferior to Governor Winthrop in breadth, in culture, and in fineness of spirit. The hot zeal, the narrow partisanship, the confident dogmatism, which characterized so much of Puritanism, have in him a striking example. No one could be more remote from the cool, skeptical, examining temper of the modern

historian, who hears, and smiles, and deducts,
and balances. All Johnson's opinions are
self-evident to him. He sees no good in the
lords bishops. He will not listen to the
servants of the chief priests; rather, his first
impulse is to draw a sword and cut off
Malchus' ear. He is full of that narrow
Hebraism which, when it prayed, kept open
its windows toward Jerusalem, but closed
every other avenue to the soul. To hew
Agag in pieces before the Lord is to his
mind not the least attractive of religious
duties. With him the church militant is
more than a metaphor. The life of the colony appears to him most frequently in the
guise of an armed conflict; he hears in its
story the noise of battle, the thunder of the
captains and the shouting, and in vehement
canticles summons the Israel of New England to the help of the Lord against the
mighty. Old Testament phrases are his
delight; he speaks, throughout, the dialect
which the French wittily call the *patois de
Canaan*. To the Puritan zeal he adds the
Puritan superstition. Everywhere the hand
of the Lord is seen protecting his saints;
his wonder-working Providence appears not
only in the general movement of the events

narrated, but in every detail of the fortunes
and misfortunes of individuals, so that his
pages bristle with special providences.   His
account of one of these may be quoted : —

"To end this yeare 1639, the Lord was
pleased to send a very sharp winter, and
more especially in strong storms of weekly
snows, with very bitter blasts; And here the
Reader may take notice of the sad hand
of the Lord against two persons, who were
taken in a storme of snow, as they were
passing from Boston to Roxbury, it being
much about a mile distant, and a very plaine
way. One of Roxbury sending to Boston
his servant maid for a Barber-Chirurgion to
draw his tooth, they lost their way in their
passage between, and were not found till
many dayes after, and then the maid was
found in one place, and the man in another,
both of them frozen to death; in which sad
accident, this was taken into consideration
by divers people, that this barber was more
than ordinary laborious to draw men to those
sinfull Errors, that were formerly so frequent, and now newly overthrowne by the
blessing of the Lord, ... he having a fit
opportunity, by reason of his trade, so soone
as they were set downe in his chaire, he
2*

would commonly be cutting of their haire
and the truth together ; notwithstanding
some report better of the man, the example
is for the living, the dead is judged of the
Lord alone."

This last is a redeeming touch. It cannot
be said that it is not in some degree characteristic. With all the illiberality and harshness of his theological zeal, the man was not
unkindly. Something of the spirit of Winthrop appeared in even the less enlightened
of those who followed him; Johnson's Puritanism was not all unlovely, and at any rate
it was far from ignoble. Let us be just to
the Puritans. Doubtless they would not be
agreeable neighbors. Doubtless they would
have hanged or burned a considerable number of us, and banished all the rest ; for in
these degenerate days hardly any one is
orthodox according to their standards. Yet
let us remember that they did possess, in
an eminent degree, those virtues that spring
from confidence in a high purpose and a
mission felt to be momentous and sacred,
from belief in character, from belief in enthusiasm, from belief in strenuous effort. If
the bit of quaint superstition which has been
quoted is characteristic of Johnson and his

companions, not less characteristic is the following passage, in which is exhibited in an instructive manner the attitude of the struggling colony toward its cherished college. Describing the eager desire of the colonists that learning should be adequately maintained among them, he says : "And verily had not the Lord been pleased to furnish N. E. with means for the attainment of learning, the work would have been carried on very heavily, and the hearts of godly parents would have vanish'd away with heaviness for their poor children, whom they must have left in a desolate wilderness, destitute of the meanes of grace." After picturesquely setting forth their sense of the magnitude of such an enterprise as the foundation of a college in comparison with their feeble resources, he goes on to say : —

"Hereupon all those who had tasted the sweet wine of Wisdom's drawing, and fed on the dainties of knowledg, began to set their wits a work. . . . Means they know there are, many thousands uneyed of mortal man, which every daies Providence brings forth; upon these resolutions, to work they go, and with thankful acknowledgement, readily take up all lawful means as they

come to hand, for place they fix their eye
upon New Town, which to tell their Posterity whence they came, is now named Cam-
bridg, and withal to make the whole world
understand, that spiritual learning was the
thing they chiefly desired, to sanctifie the
other, and make the whole lump holy, and
that learning being set upon its right object,
might not contend for error instead of truth;
they chose this place, being then under the
Orthodox, and soul-flourishing Ministry of
Mr. Thomas Shepheard. . . . The scitua-
tion of this colleg is very pleasant, at the end
of a spacious plain, more like a bowling-
green, then a wilderness, neer a fair navi-
gable river, environed with many Neighboring Towns of note, . . . the building
thought by some to be too gorgeous for a
wilderness, and yet too mean in others appre-
hensions for a colleg, it is at present inlar-
ging by purchase of the neighbour houses, it
hath the conveniences of a fair Hall, com-
fortable Studies, and a good Library, given
by the liberal hand of some Magistrates
and Ministers with others.   The chief gift
towards the founding of this Colledg, was by
Mr. John Harvard, a reverend Minister; the
country being very weak in their publike

Treasury, expended about 500. £ toward it,
and for the maintenance thereof, gave the
yearly revenue of a Ferry passage between
Boston and Charlestown, the which amounts
to about 40. or 50. £ per annum. . . .
This Colledg hath brought forth, and nurst
up very hopeful plants, to the supplying
some churches here, as the gracious and
godly Mr. Wilson, son to the grave and
zealous servant of Christ, Mr. John Wilson,
[and others]. . . . Mr. Henry Dunster is
now president of [it], fitted from the Lord
for the work, and by those that have skill
that way reported to be an able Proficient,
in both Hebrew, Greek, and Latine languages, an Orthodox preacher of the truths
of Christ, very powerful through his blessing to move the affection; and besides he
having a good inspection into the well-or-
dering of things for the Students' maintenance (whose commons hath been very short
hitherto) by his frugal providence hath continued them longer at their studies than
otherwise they could have done; and, verily,
it's great pity such ripe heads as many of
of them be, should want means to further
them in learning."

One curious feature of Johnson's style of

historical composition remains to be noted.
This is his habit of inserting in his narrative
bits of original verse. The earliest colonial
writers were somewhat addicted to this habit.
Roger Williams closes each short chapter of
his Indian grammar, or "Key into the Language of America," with a stanza or so of
verses as bad as any that one often encounters; John Smith, we have seen, developed
in later life something of this habit. But
few among them all had it in a more aggra-
vated form than the author of the "Wonder-
Working Providence." His book contains
no less than sixty-eight poems. The present
writer has read them all, with the pious care
of a lineal descendant, and can confidently
state that they are all very bad. One of
them, on the Massachusetts Company, runs in
this unconsciously brisk and jaunty manner :

"For richest Jems and gainfull things most Merchants
    wisely venter;
Deride not then New England men, this Corporation
    enter;
Christ calls for Trade shall never fade, come Craddock
    factors send;
Let Mayhew go and other more, spare not thy coyne to
    spend;
Such Trades advance did never chance, in all thy Trading
    yet,
Though some deride thy losse, abide, her 's gaine beyond
    man's wit."

Most of them, however, are in honor or
commemoration of individual persons pro-
minently concerned in the foundation of the
colony, or godly ministers of its churches.
The author, after mentioning the person,
inserts some modest introductory phrase,
such as, " of whom the author is bold to say
as followeth," or " in remembrance of whom
mind this meeter," and then, to use a phrase
now become classic, " drops into poetry."
One of the most characteristic is that which
ensues after the mention of Governor John
Endicott. " And now," he says, " let no
man be offended at the author's rude verse,
penned of purpose to keepe in memory the
names of such worthies as Christ made
strong for himselfe, in this unwonted worke
of his."

" Strong valiant John wilt thou march on, and take up
    station first,
Christ cal'd hath thee, his soldier be, and faile not of thy
    trust;
Wilderness wants Christ's grace supplants, then plant
    his Churches pure,
With Tongues gifted, and graces led, help thou to his
    procure;
Undaunted thou wilt not allow, Malignant men to wast:
Christs Vineyard heere, whose grace should cheere, his
    well-beloved's tast.
Then honoured be, thy Christ hath thee their Generall
    promoted :

To show their love, in place above, his people have thee
    voted.
Yet must thou fall, to grave with all the Nobles of the
    Earth,
Thou rotting worme, to dust must turn, and worse but
    for new birth."

But in truth the service of Clio can hardly
be profitably mixed with the meditation of
other muses, and Johnson's book, in spite of
his "meeters" and his excellent intentions,
is not a historical source of the first quality.
For while he gives much valuable information, especially as to the successive planting
of new towns and churches in Massachusetts,
he is not seldom inaccurate.

Such were the four historians, and such
was the historiography of our first colonial
period. Of other writers, whose works were
not of purely historical import, or who attained not unto the first four, it is not my
purpose to speak. Yet one of these works,
Hubbard's "Narrative of the Indian War," a
book marked by much vividness of narration,
was in its own time esteemed of such importance that, for the perusing and approving
it, we are told, "three honorable Magistrates
were deputed by the Governor and Council
of the Massachusetts Colony (one of whom
was a Major-General, and the other two were

afterwards Governors)." The whirligig of
time brings its revenges. In our day, major-
generals and governors, and even presidential
candidates, have taken to the writing of history, and the historical scholar has the opportunity of reviewing them.

II.

THE EIGHTEENTH CENTURY.

ACCORDING to the arrangements of chronology, the seventeenth century ended with the year 1700. According to the real facts of history, the period that we always think of as the seventeenth century ended at least a dozen years earlier, and the real eighteenth century then began. In other words, though there was no violent break, yet with the fall of the House of Stuart and the formation of the Grand Alliance a new page in the history of western Europe was turned. The age of Richelieu, of Strafford, of Cromwell, and of Milton had ended; the age of Walpole, of Dubois and Fleury, of Pope and Voltaire, had already begun. A century of prose, of criticism, of wit, and of finish set in. The very wars that have been alluded to are typical of the change. The conflicts in which the preceding generations had been engaged — the Thirty Years' War, the civil wars in England and in France — were con-

flicts for great religious or constitutional
principles. The war which opened with the
formation of the Grand Alliance and the
expulsion of James II. was more like the
wars of the succeeding period, — wars not
wholly dynastic, indeed, but of a dryly
political character, and waged rather with
gallantry than with lofty enthusiasm. Politics, at any rate in England, where alone
politics was a popular concern, subsided into
a condition unenthusiastic, inanimate, and
humdrum. Material prosperity was rapidly
increasing, and the world, tired of the age
of conflict, became devoted to the pursuit of
wealth. Society settled down into that prosaic and secular temper, that engrossment
with the material elements of life, that absence of high ideals, to which of late we
have been giving the name Philistinism.
Political life consisted of little but selfish
personal conflicts, between statesmen who
laughed good-naturedly at the mention of
patriotism or public virtue. The church
was lifeless. The world was its own god,
and Sir Robert Walpole was its prophet.

The independence of Europe which America has enjoyed since the War of 1812, and
has more distinctly felt since the close of

the Civil War, inclines us sometimes to
speak and think of our earlier history as if
an equal degree of independence prevailed
in those times. The history of America is
written as a separate story, as the story of
something quite isolated. In reality, the
same waves of thought and feeling generally
agitated both, though they sometimes reached
the American shores a little later. Fashions
in these matters were as naturally followed
in the colonies as fashions in dress or in
social usages are followed in colonies everywhere. So it happened that the age of
Walpole was marked by much the same
phenomena on this side of the water as in
England. No period in our history was so
dull. Political enthusiasm, whether it were
enthusiasm for liberty or enthusiasm for loy-
alty, declined, and gave place to an unheroic
apathy. Religious zeal declined not less.
Even controversial life in the church was
concerned with matters less vital than here-
tofore; while as to controversies in matters
of state, they centred almost universally
about interests of a petty and personal and
selfish sort, so that history finds little better
to record than the quarrels of the royal governors with the colonial assemblies. The

country was growing rich and prosperous, and as it sought wealth and prosperity more and more, the intensity which had marked the preceding period rapidly relaxed. The generation grew broader and more tolerant, indeed, but it at the same time grew more worldly and more commonplace in its aims and thoughts.

The incoming of this age of prose had, I am persuaded, more unhappy results in New England than in Virginia, or in the Southern and Middle colonies generally. Its easier tone was better suited to the life and manners that had grown up in those milder and softer climates. The alteration from the seventeenth century was less marked and less demoralizing. But in Massachusetts the candid inquirer is forced to admit a deterioration for which the gain in liberality was hardly a compensation. Few things in our history are more pathetic than the grief of the uncompromising elders when the Massachusetts charter was taken away and the Puritan theocracy fell. But the succeeding generation grew accustomed to the change, and submitted themselves willingly unto Cæsar. The great experiment, the object of so much prayer and solicitude and ceaseless

effort, had failed. The strenuousness which
had arisen from high aims and devotion to a
great and religious task in part gave way, in
part became diverted into pettier channels.
The elder Puritans had shown harshness and
austerity, but mixed with these were elements
of grandeur. In the eighteenth century there
is much of the same harshness and rigor, but
the diary of Judge Sewall, the New England
Pepys, shows us minds painfully exercised
about small things, — about periwigs and sur-
plices and the observance of Christmas.

Sewall does not properly fall within the
scope of these papers. In his solemn yet
amusing way, he furnishes us with valuable
historical material, indeed, but not with a
professed historical composition. But much
the same character is borne by the most
prominent historian of the age, that redoubt-
able New England Boanerges, the Reverend
Doctor Cotton Mather, the "literary behe-
moth" of our colonial era, as Professor Tyler
has called him; author of no less than four
hundred and fifty-two published writings,
and especially of the "Magnalia Christi
Americana; or, The Ecclesiastical History
of New England, from Its First Planting in
the Year 1620, unto the Year of our Lord,

1698." This miracle of learning and piety
and factious ambition and pedantry and con-
ceit was born to every advantage which
could attend a New England historian of
the colonial period. He was the grandson
of two of the chief lights of the pulpit in
the days of the settlement, the Rev. John
Cotton and the Rev. Richard Mather. His
father, Dr. Increase Mather, was minister
of a large parish in Boston, president of
Harvard College, himself author of ninety-
two writings, and for many years the most
influential as well as the most learned man
in New England. Great things were expected of one who began life under such
auspices, — *non sine dis animosus infans.*
Cotton Mather early began to satisfy these
expectations. He was graduated from Harvard College at an age younger than that of
any bachelors save two in its whole history,
and three years later took the master's degree, sustaining in public disputation the
thesis that the Hebrew points are of divine
origin. His early piety was not less conspicuous. "When he began to speak almost," says his son and biographer, "he
began to *pray*, and practiced this Duty constantly while he was a School-Boy; and,

altho' he used no *Forms* in Secret, he composed some for his School-Fellows & obliged
them to pray. Before he could write notes
of Sermons *in public* Assemblies, he commonly wrote what he remembred when he
came home. He read the *Scriptures* with
so much *Ardor* and Assiduity, that *fifteen
Chapters* a Day divided into three Exercises, and nothing less, would suffice him.
He would moreover reprove his Play-mates
for their wicked Words and Practices." At
fourteen he began the practice of frequent
fasting.

Not many years after his graduation, this
pink of youthful priggery was called to be
assistant in his father's church, of which he
remained a pastor for nearly half a century,
for much of that time directing the affairs
of the province, like a pope, from the pulpit
of the Old North Church. His rich and
fruitful activity in public affairs during that
period cannot here be described, although
important illustrations of his character may
be derived from his course in the witchcraft
troubles, in which he was extraordinarily
active; urging on the courts to more and
more prosecutions, stimulating the popular
excitement, and making the most violent

efforts to prevent the natural reaction. It is with his literary activities and mental characteristics that we are concerned. His son, relating his death-bed conversation, says: "I asked him *what Sentence or Word, what* Πύκνον ᾽Επος, *He would have me think on constantly,* for I ever desired to have him before me and hear him speaking to me? He said, ' Remember only that one word *Fructuosus.*'" The advice was highly characteristic. Never was there a mortal of more prodigious industry. In one year he prepared and published fourteen books, preached more than seventy-two public sermons and nearly half as many private ones, kept sixty fasts and twenty-two vigils, besides attending to his other varied duties, for he was most assiduous in pastoral labors. The amount of his work in the study was enormous; that of his work among men was scarcely less so. The 361st of his works, as catalogued by Mr. Sibley, is entitled "Honesta Parsimonia; or, Time Spent as it should be. Proposals, . . . To prevent that Great Folly and Mischief, The Loss of Time." Herein, at least, the learned and painful doctor practiced what he preached. The record of the various ingenious means which

5

he employed in order not to waste any time
is an amusing and interesting one. Even
his prayers and meditations and thoughts
were carefully systematized. The topic and
method of his meditations while dressing
were prescribed for each morning in the
week. There was method observed even in
the occasional thoughts with which he strove
to have odd moments profitably occupied.

" When the Doctor waked in the *Night*,"
says his son, " he would impose it as a Law
upon Himself ever before he fell asleep
again to bring some *Glory of his Saviour*
into his Meditations, and have some agreeable *Desire of his Soul* upon it. . . . When
he *washed his Hands*, he must think of the
clean Hands, as well as *pure Heart*, which
belong to the Citizens of Zion. And when
he did so mean an Action as *paring his
Nails*, he tho't how he might *lay aside all
Superfluity of Naughtiness*. . . . He was
very constant in *Ejaculatory Prayers and
Praises*. . . . While he *walked the Streets*,
or *sat in a Room* with his Mind otherwise
unemployed, he would not lose the Time, but
use his *Wit* as well as *Grace* in contriving
some suitable *Blessing* for such and such as
were before him ; and then he would form

it into an *Ejaculation* for them. . . . When
he *walked the Streets*, he still *blessed* many
Persons who never knew it, with *secret
Wishes* after this manner for them ; Upon
the sight of a tall man, '*Lord, Give that
Man high attainments in Christianity.*'
A lame Man, '*Lord, Help that Man on
moral Accounts to walk uprightly.*' A
Negro, '*Lord, Wash that poor Soul ; make
him white by the Washing of thy Spirit.*'
A Man going by without observing him,
'*Lord, I pray Thee, Help that Man to
take a due Notice of Christ.*' " The pun-
ning habit which is here noticeable crops
out in all his writings, and indeed a general habit of verbal jingles and ingenuities
which might justify one in applying to
himself what he in the " Magnalia " says in
praise of Rev. John Wilson, and commend-
ing

"His care to guide his *flock* and feed his *lambs*,
  By *words, works, prayers, psalms, alms* and *anagrams.*"

Enough has been cited to show thoroughly
the character of this extraordinary man, —
a man of extraordinary piety, no doubt, but
also of extraordinary self-consciousness, ris-
ing at times into the most amusing vanity.
His tireless energy and industry in study

went far towards fitting him to be a historian of New England. His family connections and his prominent position gave him
additional facilities for such a task. Already,
among his multitudinous publications, he
had issued a few minor ones of historical
content, such as " The Bostonian Ebenezer,"
" Decennium Luctuosum," " Arma Virosque
Cano," and " A Pillar of Gratitude." But
about 1693 he formed the design of writing
a general church history of New England, a
design which the neighboring ministers much
encouraged. It was finished in 1697. On
January 12, 1698, he records in his diary :
" I set apart this day for the exercise of a
secret fast before the Lord. One special
design of my supplications was to obtain
the direction of Heaven about my ' Church
History,' the time and way of my sending it
into Europe, and the methods of its publication. I think I am assured that my supplications are heard in this matter." After long
delays, an opportunity occurred to send it to
London ; but still further delays intervened.
The book was large, the publishers were
cold ; but at length one was found who, not
with any expectation of gain, but for the
glory of God, undertook its publication. It

may be interesting to note the mode in which
the historian manifested his concern for his
precious work, — a mode perhaps not often
observed by the historians of our day. In
his diary, under date of April 4, 1702, oc-
curs the following entry : —

"I was in much distress upon my spirit
concerning my 'Church History,' and some
other elaborate composures, that I have sent
into London ; about the progress towards
the publication whereof the Lord still keeps
me in the dark. To have those composures,
with all my labors and all my prayers about
them, lost, would be a terrible trial to me.
But I thought it my duty to prepare for such
a trial. Wherefore I set apart a vigil this
night peculiarly for that service. Accordingly, in the dead of the night, I first sang
some agreeable psalms ; and then, casting
myself prostrate in the dust, on my study-
floor, before the Lord, I confessed unto him
the sins for which he might justly reject me
and all my services ; and I promised unto
him, that if He would reject those particular
services, which I have been laboring to do
for His name, in my 'Church History,' and
some of the composures now in England,
though my calamity therein would be very

sensible, yet I would with His help submit
patiently unto His holy will therein ; and I
would not be discouraged thereby at all from
further endeavors to serve my Lord Jesus
Christ, but I would love him still, and seek
him still, and serve him still, and never be
weary of doing so, but essay to serve him in
other ways, if he would not accept of these.
Thus did I resign unto the Lord ; who there-
upon answered me, that He was my Father,
and that He took delight in me, and that
He would smile upon my endeavors to serve
Him, and that my ' Church History ' should
be accepted and prospered."

Mather's solicitude for his books, it ought
to be said, should not be regarded as arising
solely from vanity. The desire to do good
by them seems to have been ever present
with him. From both motives, he used the
utmost care and ingenuity and diligence in
disseminating copies of them in all directions,
more especially throughout New England, as
soon as he received them from the press of
Boston or of London. The arrival of the
first copy of the " Magnalia " is thus chroni-
cled by him, October 30, 1702 : —

"Yesterday I first saw my ' Church History ' since the publication of it. A gentle-

man arrived here from Newcastle in England, that had bought it there. Wherefore
I set apart this day for solemn *thanksgiving*
unto God for his watchful and gracious
providence over that work, and for the har-
vest of so many prayers and cares and tears
and resignations as I had employed upon it.
My religious friend, Mr. Bromfield, who
had been singularly helpful to the publication of that great book (of twenty shillings
price at London), came to me at the close
of the day, to join with me in some of my
praises to God."

The offspring of all these " prayers and
cares and tears and resignations " is indeed a
large book, distended by abundant divagations
and moralizings and quotations, and even
the insertion, in extended reprint, of essays
already published. There is little consis-
tency or method in the mode of presentation. It is the outpouring of a full mind
working at great speed. The general scheme
is plain enough, but it is such as to involve
much repetition and looseness of arrangement. The first of the seven books of which
the " Magnalia " consists gives a somewhat
desultory history, not only ecclesiastical but
civil, of the colonies of New England. As an

appendix to this book is reprinted "The
Bostonian Ebenezer." The second book is
entitled "Ecclesiarum Clypei," and contains
the lives of the governors that were as shields
unto the churches of New England. To
each of the more important ones is conse-
crated a separate chapter, under some such
quaint title as "Nehemias Americanus, the
Life of John Winthrop, Esq., Governour of
the Massachuset Colony." The third book
gives, in forty-three chapters, the lives of
the principal New England divines. The
first part, entitled "Johannes in Eremo"
(John in the wilderness), commemorates four
of the most prominent, grouped together,
for no other reason, apparently, than that
they all bore the name John, — John Cotton, John Norton, John Wilson, and John
Davenport. In the second part (quaintly
entitled "Sepher Jereim, i. e. Liber Deum
Timentium; or, Dead Abels yet speaking
and spoken of"), in the third part, and in
the fourth, other clerical worthies are commemorated who were of less consequence, or
who did not have the name of John. The
fourth book is devoted to the history of
Harvard College, and the biographies of its
more eminent graduates; the fifth, to the

acts and monuments of the New England
church. The sixth book, perhaps the most
curious of all, is called "Thaumaturgus, . . .
i. e. Liber Memorabilium, . . . wherein
very many illustrious discoveries and demon-
strations of Divine Providence in remarkable Mercies and Judgments on many particular persons among the people of New
England, are observed, collected and related." One chapter, headed "Christus
super Aquas," is given to remarkable de-
liverances by sea; another, " Ceraunius or
Brontologia Sacra," to providences connected with thunder and lightning. Still
another has as an appendix a history of crim-
inals executed for capital crimes, with their
dying speeches. But the most remarkable
of all is that bearing the formidable title
"Thaumatographia Pneumatica," and "relating the wonders of the invisible world in
preternatural occurrences." "There has
been," he says, "too much cause to observe,
that the christians who were driven into the
American Desart, which is now call'd *New
England*, have to their sorrow seen *Azazel*
[Satan] dwelling and raging there in very
tragical instances. The devils have doubtless felt a more than ordinary vexation, from

the arrival of those christians with their
sacred exercises of christianity in this wilderness : But the sovereignty of heaven has
permitted them still to remain in the wilderness, for our vexation, as well as their own."
And so he proceeds to a detailed narration
of fourteen selected cases of witchcraft,
forming a chapter of most curious reading,
and a monument of his own ingenuity and
credulity. Finally, the " Magnalia " closes
with a book called " Ecclesiarum Prœlia,
or, A Book of the Wars of the Lord." It
is, however, mainly concerned with the conflicts of the colonial authorities against her-
etics ; but at the end it includes a reprint
of the two small books, " Arma Virosque
Cano " and " Decennium Luctuosum," giving an account of the Indian wars.

Such was the composition of this famous
work. Its style was not less peculiar.
Prince, indeed, in his funeral sermon upon
Mather, confesses that " in his Style indeed
He was something singular, and not so
agreable to the Gust of the Age." He was
probably the most learned man, and certainly had the largest library, in colonial
America. The treasures of these intellectual
resources were lavished upon his work, until

its tissue was heavy and stiff with the jewels
of pedantic quotation. It is a very easy
matter to appear erudite, and doubtless
Mather knew the imposing trick of jauntily
alluding to recondite authors, and ignor-
ing their unfamiliarity to writer as well as
reader. But with all deductions, he was
really very learned. The jewels were gen-
uine enough ; the fault was that the fabric
was overloaded with them. Some indeed
have breathed a suspicion that they were
out of all proportion to the value of the
ground-stuff. An eminent but crotchety
historical scholar of the last generation used
systematically to refuse to believe any un-
supported statement of Mather. This, however, is unjust. He is often inaccurate, but
he has conveyed to us a great amount of
information not elsewhere attainable. The
criticisms upon his historical style may best
be explained by showing a bit of it. With
some difficulty, I select a passage not cum-
bered with Greek and Latin quotations.
It is the beginning of the chapter called
" Venisti tandem ? or discoveries of America : " —

"It is the opinion of some, though 't is
but an *opinion,* and *but* of *some* learned

men, that when the sacred oracles of heaven
assure us, *the things under the earth* are
some of those, *whose knees are to bow in the
name of Jesus,* by those *things* are meant
the inhabitants of *America,* who are Antipodes to those of the other *hemisphere.* I
would not quote any words of *Lactantius,*
though there are some to countenance this
interpretation, because of their being so *un-
geographical.* . . . I can contentedly allow
that *America* (which as the learned *Nicolas
Fuller* observes, might more justly be called
Columbina) was altogether unknown to the
penmen of the Holy Scriptures, and in the
ages when the scriptures were penned. I
can allow, that those parts of the earth,
which do not include *America,* are in the
inspired writings of *Luke,* and of *Paul,*
stiled, *all the world.* I can allow, that the
opinion of *Torniellus,* and of *Pagius,* about
the apostles preaching the gospel in *America,* has been sufficiently refuted by *Basna-
gius.* But I am out of the reach of Pope
Zachary's excommunication. I can assert
the existence of the *American Antipodes ;*
and I can report unto the *European*
churches great occurrences among these
Americans."

Even if the Americans were antipodes of Europeans in a geographical sense, which is hardly literally true, they were far from being so in respect to mental development. One of the most interesting facts about Mather as a literary phenomenon is that he is our chief American example of a remarkable historical school then dominant in every part of Europe, and shows America participating in the life and evolution of European thought. The sixteenth century and the early seventeenth had been an age of great historians who were also great men. Prominent statesmen and soldiers wrote brilliant accounts of events in which they had borne an active part. Something of this characteristic belongs, as we have seen in the previous chapter, to the American historical writers of that time. The period from 1650 to 1750, on the other hand, was in Europe distinctively an age of erudition. Excellence in historical narrative declined, but enormous labors of investigation, criticism, and publication were carried through. It was the age of Bollandists and Benedictines, of Mabillon and Muratori and Rymer. In every country giants of erudition arose, and vast additions were made to the sum of his-

6

torical knowledge. Obviously, Cotton Mather was nowise the equal of these Anakim.
But he is their American analogue, and he,
and Thomas Prince, and the Rev. William
Stith, of Virginia, show us that already the
English colonies so far shared the life of
the world that even the movements of European scholarship found their counterpart on
these shores.

But there was, at any rate, one American
historian who was not thus mentally annexed
to Europe, but retained an original spirit,
racy of the Virginian soil. It has already
been remarked that the incoming of the age
of Walpole had less undesirable effects in
Virginia than in New England. Something
must be attributed to the happier influence
of the climate ; something, to origin from
Englishmen whose traditions were not Puritan. But whatever were the causes, the tone
of Virginia life and thought in the earlier
part of the eighteenth century was an exceedingly attractive one. The tone of Virginia life, I ought perhaps rather to say ; for
of its thought we really know little. But
its life, at any rate, was marked by an open-
ness, a freshness, a geniality, strikingly con-
trasting with the narrow strenuousness which

the decline of Puritan fervor had left behind
it in contemporary Massachusetts. The
Virginian planters were not less worldly
and unheroic, not less the children of the
eighteenth century. But their engrossment
with the world took the turn of a hearty
delight in it, so fresh and spontaneous and
agreeable as half redeemed its Philistinism.
Of this life, easy-going and commonplace
and sterile of intellectual achievement, yet
pleasing and natural, we fortunately have
an admirable exponent in Robert Beverley.
Perhaps it is rather as such an exponent than
as a historian that Beverley is valuable to us;
for, excellent as his historical narration is, it
occupies but little more than a third of the
not very large book which, in 1705, he published under the title " The History of Virginia." The rest is descriptive of the natural
productions of the country, of the Indians
and their civilization, and of the present
state of the colony and the nature of its
government. It is this last portion, apparently, out of which the volume grew. In
his youth, Beverley's father was clerk of the
House of Burgesses ; he thus became familiar with the public records and public business of the colony, and for his own infor-

mation gathered many notes regarding its
administration. These notes lay unused until
the year 1703, when, after the fashion of the
wealthy planters of that day, he went to
London upon business. Soon after his arrival, his bookseller told him that a general
account of all Her Majesty's plantations in
America was being prepared for printing,
and requested him to look over that part of
it relating to Virginia and Carolina. The
book was Oldmixon's " British Empire in
America." Half a dozen sheets of the
manuscript of it were brought to Mr. Beverley. What followed may as well be related
in the colonial proprietor's own words as in
any paraphrase of them : —

" I very innocently (when I began to read)
placed Pen and Paper by me, and made my
Observations upon the first Page, but found
it in the Sequel so very faulty, and an
Abridgment only of some Accounts that had
been printed 60 or 70 years ago ; in which
also he had chosen the most strange and un-
true Parts, and left out the more sincere
and faithful, so that I laid aside all Thoughts
of farther Observations, and gave it only a
Reading ; and my Bookseller for Answer,
that the Account was too faulty and too im-

perfect to be mended : Withal telling him,
that seeing I had in my junior Days taken
some Notes of the Government, which I then
had with me in England, I would make him
an Account of my own Country, if I could
find Time, while I staid in London. And
this I should rather undertake in Justice
to so fine a Country ; because it has been
so misrepresented to the common People of
England, as to make them believe, that the
Servants in Virginia are made to draw in
Cart and Plow, as Horses and Oxen do in
England, and that the Country turns all
People black, who go to live there, with
other such prodigious Phantasms. Accordingly before I left London, I gave him a
short History of the Country, from the first
Settlement, with an Account of its then
State; but I would not let him mingle it
with Oldmixon's other Account of the Plan-
tations, because I took them to be all of a
Piece with those I had seen of Virginia and
Carolina, but desired mine to be printed by
itself."

It is no wonder that Beverley took this
course, in view of some of the errors he
signalizes in that book. For instance, in
one passage Oldmixon said, " When Indians

at the Head of the Bay [*i. e.* Chesapeake
Bay] travelled to New York, they past, going and coming, by the frontiers of Virginia
and traded with the Virginians," etc.   Here
we have, early exemplified, that originality of
view respecting American geography on the
part of Englishmen which was until recent
times the source of so much vexation to
American bosoms, and which, now that we
have become less sensitive, proves so peren-
nially amusing.

The paragraph which I have quoted to
show the genesis of Beverley's book will also
serve to exhibit the merits of his style.   It
is simple, clear, and direct, far removed from
the curious involution and cumbersome pedantry of Cotton Mather's; it never smacks
of the lamp.   The author was a plain Virginia gentleman, who had read some books,
not too many, perhaps, but did not think it
necessary to mention them all, nor to quote
them with a frequency inversely propor-
tioned to the familiarity of the language in
which they were written.   A French trav-
eler of the period has left us an interesting
picture of the home and the simple rural life
of Beverley, whom he happened to visit upon
business.   It is too long to be here quoted;

but the characteristics which it brings to
light are most attractive and Arcadian.
Again and again in Beverley's book his
strong love of nature crops out, and some
of his descriptions are truly delightful.
This, however, is in the second, third, and
fourth parts of the book. As to the first or
historical portion, it is too brief to convey to
us a very great body of information on Virginian history ; but the sprightliness and
ease of the style prevent its ever seeming
dry. For the latter years of the seventeenth
century, the years just before it was written, its volume becomes greater, and it gives
some interesting information on details of
public affairs, such as might easily come to
the writer not only from his own experience,
but from his family connections, for he was
brother-in-law at once to President John
Robinson and to Colonel Byrd of Westover.

Leaving aside such plain and business-like
accounts as that of Beverley, the histories
hitherto written in America had mostly been
written either for the glory of God, or for
the glory of the writer, as in the case of
Captain John Smith, or for the glory of
both in curious mixture, as in the case of
Cotton Mather. It remained for some one

to prepare the soil for the growth of American historical scholarship by beginning to write history without didactic or personal tendency, and in a truly scientific spirit. It may fairly be said that the wealth and leisure of the torpid and money-getting age which has been described were necessary prerequisites. The traditional view is that scholarship and poverty are twin sisters. In reality, however it may be of scholarship generally, the thorough pursuit of history requires so much laborious research, and therefore so much leisure on the part of some one, that for its successful conduct it has generally been necessary that, if not the individual, at any rate the age, should be rich. At all events, with the increase of wealth a hundred and fifty years ago, there did appear our first historical scholars, one in Virginia, one in Massachusetts. There was a curious parallelism, not only in their purposes and methods, but also in the unfortunate immediate fate of their books.

The two scholars alluded to are the Rev. Thomas Prince, minister of the Old South Church in Boston, and the Rev. William Stith, president of William and Mary College in Virginia. The elder of the two was

the Boston clergyman, a man of high and
amiable character, who from his boyhood
had possessed an eager interest in whatever
bore upon the history of New England.
Appreciating more highly than those who
had preceded him the need of scholarly
thoroughness and the value of original authorities, he spent years in making a search,
as exhaustive as he could, for printed and
manuscript materials. Thus he formed that
invaluable New England Library which has
been already more than once referred to, and
of which a considerable portion, surviving
to our times, forms the priceless Prince Collection in the Boston Public Library. Of
books, pamphlets, and printed papers he had
accumulated, he tells us, about a thousand;
he had also gathered together a multitude of
manuscripts left by the early settlers, documents, copies, and letters, to the number of
several hundred.

With these copious materials, Prince at
length, though with diffidence, began the
composition of a Chronological History of
New England. His modest aim did not ex-
tend to the preparation of a historical composition in the fullest sense; he proposed
merely to write a chronology, but with every

sort of care to secure the most minute accuracy. He proposed to include " remarkable providences," the deaths of prominent
men, brief notices of transactions of the government, elections, grants and settlement of
towns, the formation of churches, the ordi-
nation and removal of ministers, the erec-
tion of important buildings, remarkable laws,
executions, wars, battles, — in short, all the
events of the earlier history of those colonies in which his contemporaries might feel
an interest. In the long introductory portion he notes down, in true annalistic fashion, the principal events in the history of the
world from its creation down to the settlement of New England. This, he confesses,
gave him a vast amount of trouble; and
we must regret that he spent so much time
in perfecting it, for the result was that the
New England Chronology never got beyond
the year 1633. Indeed, the first volume,
published in 1736, carried the narrative no
farther than to the autumn of 1630. Here
the publication rested until eighteen or nine-
teen years later, when the author, then an
old man, began the publishing of volume
second by the issue of sixpenny numbers,
of thirty-two pages each. Only three such

numbers, it is supposed, were ever issued;
and of these three no one now possesses a
perfect set. The truth seems to be, that
there was not at that time an adequate public demand for a history so minute as Prince
provided.

It will be evident from the plan of his
work that it does not lend itself readily to
interesting quotation. But it is the first of
our histories, not itself an original source,
which is of value as a contribution to historical science rather than to historical literature ; and it is to this that it owes its great
importance. Prince and his Virginian contemporary are the progenitors of modern
American historiography. The wide sweep
of the search after materials, the patience
and industry in investigation, the minute
accuracy and fidelity which characterize the
best of the moderns, are all to be found
in Prince, and to be found in a high degree.
"It is Exactness I aim at," he says, "and
would not have the least mistake, if possible,
pass to the world. If I have unhappily fallen
into any, it is through inadvertency only."
The spirit of the work, it will be seen, was
that of the Benedictines of St. Maur ; and
the execution seems to have been as scholarly
as the intention.

Among the points of resemblance between Prince and Stith, their ill-success in publication is one of the most remarkable, and in truth not at all creditable to our forefathers. There is something highly amusing in the tone of annoyance with which Stith remarks the indifference of his contemporaries to his labors. After speaking of his intention to have included many more interesting documents, he says : " But I perceive, to my no small Surprise and Mortification, that some of my Countrymen (and those too, Persons of high Fortune and Distinction) seemed to be much alarmed, and to grudge, that a complete History of their own Country would run to more than one Volume, and cost them above half a Pistole. I was, therefore, obliged to restrain my Hand, . . . for fear of enhancing the Price, to the immense Charge and irreparable Damage of such generous and publick-spirited Gentlemen." This, we may suppose, was the reason why the work was never carried beyond the year 1624. If it had been carried down, on the same scale, to the year of publication, 1747, it would have made an eight-volume history of the colony of Virginia, a work of such bulk that even " Persons of High Fortune and Distinction " in Virginia might be excused for hesitating to support it.

Yet these persons might have done well to sustain him, for his " History of the First Discovery and Settlement of Virginia " is an excellent piece of work, — pleasing in style, accurate, and fair. That it is too prolix, however, is a thing that cannot be denied ; and this is the more to be blamed because the proportions between the different parts show us clearly that the author was dominated by his materials, rather than master of them, and that he relates much of his story at great length simply because it is in his power to do so. Thus, out of the seventeen years which he treats, he devotes three fourths of his space to the first three years and the last five, evidently because materials were most abundant for these. For the years 1607–1609 he could draw on the most detailed portion of Captain John Smith's narrative, — a source the complete trustworthiness of which he seems in general not at all to doubt, though disposed to make considerable allowances for personal pique and party spirit in regard to Smith's expressions concerning the Virginia Company. " Not," he says, " that I question Captain

7

Smith's Integrity; for I take him to have been a very honest Man, and a strenuous Lover of Truth."

When this esteemed guide leaves him, the ex-president of William and Mary falls back upon the papers in the Capitol at Williamsburg, and the collection of documents made, for historical purposes, by his late uncle, Sir John Randolph. With the year 1619, however, his narrative widens into a very copious account, which is derived, in a far greater degree than has been generally supposed hitherto, from one of the sources which he mentions. The mode in which he refers to it is as follows: " But I must confess myself most indebted, in this Part of my History, to a very full and fair Manuscript of the London Company's Records, which was communicated to me by the late worthy President of our Council, the Honorable William Byrd, Esq." The records so described have a curious history, and one which, it may be remarked parenthetically, authors have almost invariably related incorrectly. In 1624 King James I. seized the papers of the company and dissolved it. Shortly before this, in anticipation of such a seizure, certain officers of the company had secretly caused

to be prepared an attested copy of the records of its proceedings during the last
five years, to serve as evidence for their
justification in case of prosecution. The
copy, when completed, was entrusted to the
president of the company, Shakespeare's
friend, the Earl of Southampton. On the
death of his son, the Lord High Treasurer
Southampton, in 1667, the two volumes of
the copy were bought of his executors, for
sixty guineas, by Captain William Byrd,
of Virginia, and for more than a century
formed a part of the extensive library of the
Byrd family at Westover. These are the
two volumes of which Stith made use, and
he appears to have used them very freely.
All subsequent historians have referred to
them, but to all appearances they have not
really used them. It would take too long to
relate how most of them passed into the possession of Thomas Jefferson, and then into
that of Congress. In the Library of Congress these primary sources for the history
of our first colony have now been buried for
sixty years, and all efforts to make them
public have hitherto failed before the apathy
of Congress and the difficulties presented by
its cumbrous machinery. Extracts from a
copy have lately been printed.

The fifth work to be mentioned, the best of all, was written by a man of conspicuous station, — lieutenant - governor, chief justice, and finally governor of Massachusetts, — and was bodily associated with a striking event in our Revolutionary history. The book referred to is the history of the colony and province of Massachusetts by Thomas Hutchinson, the famous Tory governor. The scene alluded to was in the time of the Stamp Act troubles, when already the first volume of the history had appeared. A Boston mob, of the sort which in our school-days we are taught to venerate as gatherings of liberty-loving patriots engaged in resisting oppression, attacked the lieutenant-governor's house. The fact was that he had disapproved of the Stamp Act policy, and had opposed it by every legal means. But liberty-loving patriots engaged in resistance to oppression cannot be expected to give attention to defenses so subtle. They broke in the doors and windows, demolished all the furniture in the house, and destroyed or scattered all the books and papers of the occupant. A clerical neighbor made efforts to save these last, and nearly all of the invaluable manuscript of the second vol-

ume of the history was thus preserved. Although it had lain in the street, scattered
abroad several hours in the rain, yet so much
of it was legible that the author was able
to supply the rest, and to transcribe it. In
spite of the loss of materials, the second
volume was published nine years later. " I
pray God," says the writer in his preface,
after speaking of the riot, " to forgive the
actors in and advisers of this most savage
and inhuman injury, and I hope their posterity will read with pleasure and profit what
has so narrowly escaped the outrage of their
ancestors." It is well known that in this
same year the governor retired to England,
from which he never returned. Long afterwards, and years after he had died in exile,
his grandson, at the request of the Massachusetts Historical Society, published the
third volume of the history. The recent
publication of his " Diary and Letters " has
made clear, to a generation more disposed to
be just to those who were faithful to their
king, that Governor Hutchinson was, both
in patriotism and in character, fully the
equal of his opponents. Of his qualities as
a historian there is but one opinion. He
was industrious in research, and had access

to many materials, especially those collected
by Cotton Mather, for Mather's son was his
brother-in-law. He wrote with excellent
judgment, and in a good though not brilliant style. " His mind," says the late Dr.
Deane, " was eminently a judicial one ; and
candor, moderation, and a desire for truth
appear to have guided his pen." Even the
third volume, which treats of the period from
1749 to 1774, the period in which he was
himself so large a figure in the bitter political contests which led to the Revolution, is
written with much fairness. The spirit with
which Hutchinson approached the history
of the colony and province is shown by a
note found among his papers, and written
near the end of his life, in which he says : —

" In the course of my education, I found
no part of science a more pleasing study
than history, and no part of the history of
any country more useful than that of its
government and laws. The history of Great
Britain and its dominions was of all others
the most delightful to me, and a thorough
knowledge of the nature and constitution of
the supreme and of the subordinate governments thereof I considered as what would be
peculiarly beneficial to me in the line of life

upon which I was entering ; and the public employments to which I was early called, and sustained for near thirty years together, gave me many advantages for the acquisition of this knowledge."

Here again, as in the case of Cotton Mather and Prince, we may suggest a parallel with the European movements. Hutchinson's approach to historical study was mainly from the point of view of the student of institutional history. In Europe, by the middle of the eighteenth century, the age of erudition had been succeeded by an age mainly devoted to the study of the development of institutions. The Puritan Hutchinson was in his way a member of the school of Montesquieu, Turgot, and Voltaire, — a disciple, consciously or unconsciously, of the " Essai sur les Mœurs."

III.

FROM THE REVOLUTION TO THE CIVIL WAR.

It is difficult to make any general statement concerning the relation which great national crises bear to the development of literature as a whole, or of historical literature in particular. Sometimes, after a nation has passed through a period of struggle, the same mental energy which has carried it through the conflict bursts forth into great literary activity. Sometimes such a period is followed by a time of silence, as if the national forces had been exhausted in military and political effort. In the case of wars for freedom and independence, however, it is generally the former which happens; for, however great the losses of war, the gain of liberty and of opportunity for free expansion is felt to be far more than a compensation, and the sense of freedom gives a freshness and spontaneity that urge toward literary expression. Thus the French Revolution, unfettering all the forces of the

national life, brought on a period of activity
in historical production more remarkable
than any since the sixteenth century, and
one noteworthy in general literary activity.
The same is in a very high degree true of
the heroic and successful struggle of the
Netherlanders for freedom. No period in
the history of Dutch literature is more brilliant than that which followed the virtual
securing of freedom by the Twelve Years'
Truce, — a period made brilliant not only by
the work of the best poets of the nation, but
also by that of some of its best scholars and
historians.

In the United States, no movement so
noteworthy resulted from the successful ac-
complishment of the War for Independence.
Not much literature of considerable value,
historical or other, appeared during or immediately after the Revolution. One reason,
no doubt, was that crudity of life and thought
which is inevitable to the colonial state ; the
country was too young and too immature to
make it reasonable to expect a great literature. And yet it is to be remembered that,
in the period just preceding, so very creditable a piece of work as Hutchinson's " History of Massachusetts Bay " had appeared,

giving promise of good things in literature
and history. Nor is it an adequate explanation to adduce the undoubtedly great losses
which Tory emigration had brought to the
classes most likely to be interested in literary development and to further it.

The truth seems to be that, by great and
perhaps premature efforts to secure independence, the States had become exhausted
to such a degree that the eventual acquisition of freedom, though hailed with loud
rejoicings, could not have, upon a people
wearied, discordant, and drained of their
resources, the vivifying effect which such
achievements are wont to have. If one keeps
in mind only the year 1776, he will think of
the Revolutionary era as a period of national
glory; but if he takes into consideration the
year 1786, and such incidents as Shays's
Rebellion, he will see that at its close the
condition of the thirteen bodies politic was
far from sound, even though independence
had at length been secured. Even the union
of 1789 did not at once bring on a healthier
state. It was entered into with reluctance,
and it was followed by discord. Alexander
Hamilton, the young Federalist Rehoboam,
laid upon the necks of an unwilling people

the yoke of a national consolidation which
their fathers had never borne. Availing
himself of the general uneasiness, like the
wily Jeroboam, the son of Nebat, his astute
opponent, Jefferson, summoning discontented
Israel to its tents, erected at ancient Beer-
sheba and newly settled Dan the golden
calves of the Virginia and Kentucky Resolutions, and through their worship prolonged
the congenial Separatism which had de-
scended to this generation from its predeces-
sors. The Revolutionary and Napoleonic
wars in Europe delayed still longer the advent of internal tranquillity.

Nevertheless, the years that intervened
between the first and the second war with
Great Britain were not wholly barren.
Something of literature began to grow up,
though the flowers that blossomed in the
prim and formal inclosures of the " Monthly
Anthology" and the "Portfolio" seem to our
eyes but a pale and sickly product. Even
for history something was being done. The
events of the Revolution, still fresh in remembrance, were commemorated in several
histories, of which one, at least, — that written by the Rev. William Gordon, — was of
great excellence. Biographies of those who

had taken a leading part in its events, such
as Chief Justice Marshall's celebrated " Life
of Washington," were in several instances
written with so much care and information
that they are among the most important
historical authorities for the story of the
War for Independence. Often, indeed, those
earlier lives have for the student of to-day
much more of the attraction of freshness
and originality than the biographies written
in our own time ; the writers of these latter
have frequently so full a sense of the American political history of which their subject
forms a part that the individuality of the
portrait is impaired by the attention paid to
the background.

There was also a third class of historical
works, to which, in the first years of the republic, important contributions were made.
To our minds, the great glory of that period
seems manifestly to be the attainment of
national independence and national union.
To the man of that day, inhabitant of a particular State, and little accustomed to "think
continentally," as the phrase was, the thought
that his colony had become an independent
and sovereign State was often quite as prominent, and was a source of pride and inspira-

tion to a degree difficult for us to conceive.
So it was that all at once, in several of the
newly fledged States, zealous and sometimes
able hands undertook the task of writing
their histories. Several such works, of various degrees of merit, appeared during the
interval between the two wars. Within two
or three years after the conclusion of peace,
David Ramsay, a doctor in Charleston, and
member of the Continental Congress, published a history of South Carolina during
the Revolutionary War, followed later by a
history of the colony and State from the
beginning, which has enjoyed and deserved
a good reputation. Another ex-member of
Congress, Hugh Williamson, published in
1812 a history of North Carolina. In 1804
came a history of Virginia by an Irish jour-
nalist in that State, John Daly Burk. It
cannot be highly praised. But the success
of a book so extensive (four vōlumes) shows
that, in that commonwealth and elsewhere,
interest in history had advanced greatly
since the time when poor Stith cut short the
superabundant product of his pen because
of inadequate support from "Persons of
high Fortune and Distinction." A few years
earlier came Robert Proud's valued "His-

8

tory of Pennsylvania," and Benjamin Trum-
bull's "History of Connecticut;" while, in
Massachusetts, George Minot wrote a continuation of Hutchinson's history; and in
Georgia, Edward Langworthy prepared a
history of that State, since lost. But the
best of them all was the Rev. Jeremy Belknap's "History of New Hampshire," which,
though published more than a hundred years
ago, has never yet been superseded. Be-
side his industry and fidelity as an investigator, Belknap had a singularly good style.
He also edited and published two volumes
of American biography, by various hands,
which were of real service to American history.

Belknap's writings, however, are not his
only, perhaps not his chief, title to recognition
by our generation. Our principal debt to
him is for his influence, which seems without
doubt to have been the dominant influence,
in founding the first of the local historical
associations of America, the Massachusetts
Historical Society, in January, 1791. This
was in some degree the beginning of a new
phase in the development of American history, though by means of the same local
channels through which, as has been said,

the current of American historical work
mostly ran during the generation succeeding
the Revolution. It was the beginning of
organized effort. The local historical societies of the present time in the United States
are in many cases far from being what we
could wish them to be. Some are lifeless,
or, like Pope and Pagan in Bunyan's alle-
gory, are toothlessly mumbling over and over
again the same innutritious materials ; some,
that seem full of activity, direct that activity toward any but the most scientific ends.
But in their day they have certainly been of
great use, and that in two ways : First, they
have heightened and fostered by association
the growing interest in American history, so
long as that interest was mostly for colonial
and local history, and until a wider interest
should prevail. The local historical society
has been, in Paul's phrase, our schoolmaster
to lead us to the general study of American
history ; the study of that national life which
in Belknap's time had hardly begun, and
which long remained latent or unattractive
to the eye of local patriotism.

In the second place, the historical societies have done good service as collectors and
publishers of historical materials. The sets

of publications of the Massachusetts Historical Society dating from 1792, and those
of the New York Historical Society dating
from 1811, are invaluable and indispensable.
We smile a little over some of the contents
of their early volumes, the remarkable articles and bits of information which our naive
great-grandfathers thought worth preserving,
but which are to us as the poke bonnets and
spinning-wheels of old garrets. But side by
side with the topographical descriptions of
towns, the copies of epitaphs, the accounts of
the northern lights, and the letters from a
gentleman recently returned from Niagara,
there is a part — and really much the larger
part — of the early work of these societies
which is still valuable. Not only was it of a
more scientific character than most of what
had preceded it, but it was of peculiar value
as establishing a certain tendency in our
historical work ; a tendency, namely, to make
the publication of materials as much an
object of the historical scholar's care as the
publication of results. The idea has, to be
sure, been slow in taking root. Even at the
present day it is but a very small part of the
population of the United States that can be
induced to believe the publication of dry

records and documents, well edited, to be
not only as useful as the publication of
interesting books of history, but, as a general rule, considerably more useful. But in
so far as the salutary notion has permeated
the public mind, that happy result has been
largely due to the wise efforts of those who,
eighty or a hundred years ago, were establishing the first local historical societies. A
zeal for the collection and preservation of
such materials at once arose, one of the first
fruits of which was the " Annals of America," which Dr. Abiel Holmes, father of Dr.
Oliver Holmes, published in 1805.

It creates some surprise to observe how
little was done in the domain of American
historical literature in the period between
the end of the first administration of Jefferson, that golden age of the young republic
and of the Democratic-Republican party, and
the times of the rule of Jackson and the new
Democracy. Especially singular, at first
sight, is the absence of activity during the
period immediately succeeding the War of
1812 ; for, as has already been observed, such
activity commonly ensues upon wars which
have had an inspiring effect upon the national consciousness. The War of 1812 was

anything but glorious, so far as military
events were concerned. But, for all that,
the popular consciousness was not mistaken
in obtaining from it a powerful stimulus to
national feeling. Its great result, unmen-
tioned though it was in the Treaty of Ghent,
was the immediate emancipation of the
United States from colonial dependence on
Europe, and from the colonial ideas which
still lingered in their politics, and the securing to them of opportunity for unlimited
development, on their own lines, of freedom
to live their own life.

How profoundly the national consciousness was affected by the opportunity and the
responsibility of working out its own salva-
tion may be seen even in the boastful confidence, the crude elation, the vociferous
patriotism, and the national arrogance which
were so painfully dominant in the America
of fifty or sixty years ago, and to which
we are wont to give colloquially the name
of " Fourth of July." Undoubtedly, America was inspired by the rapidly opening
prospect of a boundless career. If the characteristic historical fruits of such inspiration were absent, or at any rate not present
in any abundance, we must look for the

explanation in that rapid expansion of the
nation's material life which went on between
1815 and 1830, and of which the immense
westward emigration of those years is but a
single though a most conspicuous sign.

When historical literature did start into
new life in the United States, such of it as
was concerned with American history showed
the influence of this popular impulse; but
for a while the time of flowering seemed
to have been delayed. Usually, periods in
which party politics have become quiescent
are favorable to the growth of historical
literature; and the age of Monroe, an era
of good feeling among the people, though
one of extremely bad feeling among the
politicians, was such a period. But it should
be remembered that the impulse of the new
era was more likely to be felt by those who
were boys at the time of the War of 1812
than by their elders, and therefore would
show its effects in literature at a somewhat
later date.

As we approach the consideration of the
classical period of American historical literature, we find ourselves confronted with a
striking fact of geographical distribution.
If we tried to name the ten principal historical

writers of that period, we should find that
seven or eight of them were Massachusetts
men, of old New England families, born in
or near Boston, and graduated at Harvard
College. How are we to account for this
extraordinary localization of our science?
Of course there are those general causes
which produced the remarkable fertility of
New England in good literature at that time,
and made Boston for so long a period our
literary centre, — the greater prevalence of
urban life in New England; the indelible
intensities of Puritan blood; the inherited
traditions of a capital city continuously literary from its origin, and of our oldest college ; the stimulating influence of the recent
Unitarian revolt, and the resulting controversies ; that leaven of buoyant energy in
political and literary thought which infused
the world in or about the revolutionary year
1830 ; and other such general causes. But
more special explanations are required, for
in the case of other sciences and branches of
learning we do not find such a proportion
obtaining. The other muses were not thus
partial to that one city and region; for
instance, if political economy has a muse,
she was not. Doubtless, something was due

to the presence of libraries. History is perhaps more dependent upon these than any other of the departments of literature or science then studied. Large libraries could be found only in those parts of the country where there were cities, and Boston and Cambridge, side by side, with the libraries of the Boston Athenæum and of Harvard College, and later the Boston Public Library, were of all our cities the best provided in this respect. Here, therefore, it might have been expected that historians would congregate, and it has been so. There is one spot of a few acres in Cambridge upon which three of the most eminent historical scholars of the last generation dwelt, and on which have dwelt three of the most prominent historical writers of our own time.

But there was still another reason why history should spring up and flourish in New England, and that was a political one. Throughout our political history we have had two parties which, under various names, have preserved an essential identity. They are usually described as the party of loose construction and the party of strict construction. This is describing them with reference to their attitude toward the Constitution only. A more penetrating analysis will discover in them the party of political measures and the party of political principles, — a party with a programme and a party with a creed. The Democratic party, during its long history, has been mainly marked by its adherence to a certain definite set of political principles. The average American citizen, in quiet times, has had no other political platform than those principles, and has therefore remained a member of the Democratic party. But from time to time there has arisen, out of this mass of Americans unanimous in adhesion to American political principles, a body of men eventually constituting a great party, united in devotion to some great political measure or set of measures, in effort, that is, to alter or add to our political fabric. The Federalist party arose, with a strong sense of work to be done, made its contribution by cementing the Union more firmly, and subsided into the mass of Democracy. With other purposes, but still with purposes of contribution and of alteration, the Whig party arose, did its work, and dissolved. Still a third time, the desire for measures restricting slavery and consolidating still more firmly the national Union drew together a great party which has left its impress indelibly upon our national institutions. Parties marked by this devotion to given political measures will infallibly be loose-constructionist in their view of the fundamental document, as will any body of men, acting under a given instrument, whose main desire is to get certain specific things done; the party of political principles meanwhile adheres to a strict construction.

Now there must of necessity be a radical difference between these two, and between any two bodies of population in which they are respectively dominant, in regard to their attitude toward history. The abstract principles of political philosophy may be supposed to remain ever the same. To the purely legal view of the strict-constructionist, based on these principles, the fundamental relations of politics remain unchanged. That which was the Constitution in 1789 is the Constitution in 1891; and what it is, is to be found by logical reasoning from political principles. The advocate of a programme of measures, of political change, on the other hand, will be constantly recurring to notions of development. To the practical aims which are foremost in his mind, the study of human experience will be of the most direct service, and he and his will incline to historical ways of thinking and to historical studies. It is not an accident that the founder of the Democratic party, with all his interest in science, in philosophy, and in the theory of politics, was but little addicted to the study of history; while his rival, the first Federalist President, was, of all the statesmen of his time and country, the most learned in that department.

To come, then, to the application. Our explanation of the concentration of historical science in the northeastern corner of our country is, in addition to the general reasons for its literary fertility, that the political predilections of the region were such as made the study of human history natural and congenial there. As New England was the chief seat of the Federalist, the Whig, and the Republican parties, the chosen abode of loose construction, it was natural that it should also be the chosen abode of historical science; for no man can escape sharing the interests which political or economical conditions have made most vivid in those around him. We may be confirmed in our view by observing that, in respect to writings of a purely political or economical character, the superiority of the South in both quantity and quality was no less incontestable. As for Massachusetts in especial, it may be observed that in a State where public spirit has always been so strong, — in other words, in a State where the interests and life of the community have been so highly regarded by individuals, — a deep interest in the life and the progressive development of communities is likely to follow.

But before passing to the consideration of our principal schools of classical historians, it may be well to say a word concerning one who belongs to neither North or South, — Washington Irving. We need not speak of him at great length, for his strictly historical works were few, and his fame was mainly achieved in other walks of literature. Nor did he have a great influence upon the development of historical writing among us, unless in the way of general influence upon American style. In fact, it is quite possible that no one of his mature and sober pieces of writing had as much real effect on the progress of American historiography as the admirable humorous composition with which he began, as far back as 1809, — the " His-

9

tory of New York" by Dietrich Knicker-
bocker. Aside from its striking success as
a literary production, the book had a great
effect in awakening interest in the early or
Dutch period of New York history. Descendants rushed with sober indignation to
the defense of ancestors at whom the genial
humorist poked his fun, and very likely the
great amount of work which the state government in the next generation did for the
historical illustration of the Dutch period,
through the researches of Mr. Brodhead in
foreign archives, had this unhistorical little
book for one of its principal causes. But,
on the other hand, he made it permanently
difficult for the American public to take a
serious view of those early Dutch days.
Oloffe the Dreamer and Walter the Doubter,
Abraham with the ten breeches and Stuyve-
sant with the wooden leg, have become too
thoroughly domesticated among us to admit
of that.

In 1828 appeared the "Life and Voyages
of Columbus." The short time in which it
was prepared, not more at any rate than two
years, shows that it cannot have been a work
of original research carried out absolutely
after the modern manner. It was in fact

based on the documentary publications of
Don Martin Fernandez de Navarrete, though
with much use of the libraries of Obadiah
Rich, then our consul at Madrid, of Navarrete himself, of the Duke of Veragua, and
of the Council of the Indies, and of other
libraries at Madrid and Seville. The result
was an excellent piece of historical work, as
well as a literary production which it would
be superfluous to praise. At about the same
time the author proposed a series of writings
on the Arabs in Spain, beginning with some
account of Mohammed himself. The fruit
of this project, the book entitled "Mahomet
and his Successors," made no pretensions to
original research, and appeared, as did the
"Life of Washington," many years after the
period which we have been considering.

The very fact that we pass over books not
based on original research shows of itself
that the period which we are approaching
was one marked by higher ideals of historical scholarship than had prevailed before.
When this classical period of American historical writing does arrive, it is found to
be marked from the first by two separate
tendencies; there are, we may almost say,
two schools, distinct throughout the period.

On the one hand, we have the historians who have devoted themselves to picturesque themes lying outside the history of the United States, — men whose traditions and associations have been mainly literary, of whom Prescott, Motley, and Parkman are the types. On the other hand, there are the historians who have interested themselves in American affairs, whose associations and impulses have in many cases been in a great degree political, but who have been more especially the inheritors of those impulses already spoken of as marking the early years of the century. The chief example of this last division is George Bancroft, whose honored life was so exceptionally prolonged that he was enabled to give to one great work the labor of fifty years, an experience unexampled in the annals of historical literature. The first volume of his " History of the United States " was published in 1834 ; the author's last revision was put forth in 1883 ; and he died but a few months ago, at the age of ninety, having lived almost as many years as Ranke, and with as severe an industry.

If we speak of the product of his long period of labor in connection with the date of its commencement rather than of its close,

it is because the work, from its very beginning, has not ceased to bear some marks of
an origin in the year 1834. At that time
Mr. Bancroft was thirty-four years old.
Graduated early from Harvard, he had next
had the privilege of university training in
Germany. This was in those days a very
unusual opportunity. It is amusing to read
of the difficulties which, at the modern
Athens itself, George Ticknor encountered
in 1813 in preliminary movements toward
a course of study at Göttingen. " I was
sure," he relates, " that I should like to
study at such a university, but it was in vain
that I endeavored to get farther knowledge
upon the subject. I would gladly have prepared for it by learning the language I
should have to use there, but there was no
one in Boston who could teach me. . . . Nor
was it possible to get books. I borrowed a
Meidinger's Grammar, French and German,
from my friend Mr. Everett, and sent to
New Hampshire, where I knew there was
a German Dictionary, and procured it. I
also obtained a copy of Goethe's ' Werther,'
in German, . . . from amongst Mr. J. Q.
Adams's books, deposited by him, on going
to Europe, in the Athenæum," etc.

This was in 1813, and it cannot have been much different in 1818, when Bancroft went to Göttingen. The two years spent there seem to have been given to quite general studies. In such studies as were historical, it is not to be thought that in the days before Ranke had appeared, and before any permanent work of Niebuhr had been published, it was possible to find in Germany such inspiration for historical studies as in times more recent, even had the young American yet resolved upon such studies. What could be obtained was a much better knowledge of methods and results than America afforded. Of those historians under whom Bancroft studied, Heeren, Savigny, Schlosser, one cannot in his History find trace of much influence, except that Heeren's interest in the history of colonies and of their reflex action upon the mother country probably bore fruit later. Of method he may have earned much from these teachers; his ideas were derived elsewhere, and mainly, in truth, from the soil from which they sprang. They are the ideas of America in the year 1834. The extraordinary popularity of the early volumes can be accounted for only in view of this fact. For the popularity of the later

volumes, it is not necessary to resort to any
other explanation than that of the enormous
amount of labor and care expended on them,
the very unusual facilities in respect to access to archives and masses of correspondence which the author's diplomatic positions
afforded him, and the encyclopædic fullness and minuteness of his knowledge of
his subject. But for the earlier volumes
these explanations fail us. If they surpassed
in research and scientific value the average
of that time, they were still not highly remarkable in those respects. And yet the
tenth edition of the first volume was published within ten years of the date of the
original edition. The book at once took
rank as the standard history of the United
States. Thousands and thousands of copies
have since been sold. At Washington, upon
the doors of the Senate and House of Re-
presentatives, its writer's name has long appeared, almost the sole name of a private
person in the brief list of those to whom
our legislative bodies have given the privilege of entrance upon their floors.

Whence did this immediate and un-
bounded popularity and acceptance arise?
Mainly, I believe, from the fact that the his-

torian caught, and with sincere and enthusiastic conviction repeated to the American
people, the things which they were saying
and thinking concerning themselves. One
need not imitate the professional scorn of
the Pharisee and declare that the people
that knoweth not the esoteric law is cursed,
and yet may freely hold the opinion that
the popularity of a work of national history
does not depend on the profundity and skill
of its research, nor on the correctness and
completeness of its results, nor even on its
qualities of arrangement and style, so much
as on the acceptableness to the national
mind of the general idea which it exhibits
in regard to the nation's development. Bancroft's first volume succeeded mainly because
it was redolent of the ideas of the new
Jacksonian democracy, — its exuberant confidence, its uncritical self-laudation, its op-
timistic hopes. The Demos heard, as an
undercurrent to his narrative, the same
music which charmed its ears in the Fourth
of July oration ; indeed, many of Bancroft's
most characteristic ideas are to be found in
his own oration pronounced at Northampton
on July 4, 1826 ; and the style was one whose
buoyancy of rhetoric was well suited to those

sanguine times. It would be but a shallow
criticism that should see in all this only the
ebullition of national vanity. The uncritical patriotism of those times, as of other
times in the course of history, was in some
respects admirable, and in many respects
useful. But we need not forget that it *was*
uncritical. The opening words of the intro-
duction to the book will serve as well as any
to exhibit what is meant : —

" The United States of America [it be-
gins] constitute an essential portion of a
great political system, embracing all the civ-
ilized nations of the earth. [This bears the
stamp of Heeren's ideas.] At a period when
the force of moral opinion is rapidly increasing, they have the precedence in the practice and the defense of the equal rights of
man. The sovereignty of the people is here
a conceded axiom, and the laws, established
upon that basis, are cherished with faithful
patriotism. While the nations of Europe
aspire after change, our Constitution en-
gages the fond admiration of the people by
which it has been established. . . . Our government, by its organization, is necessarily
identified with the interests of the people,
and relies exclusively on their attachment

for its durability and support. Even the enemies of the state, if there are any among us, have liberty to express their opinions undisturbed, and are safely tolerated where reason is left free to combat their errors. Nor is the Constitution a dead letter, unalterably fixed; it has the capacity for improvement, adopting whatever changes time and the public will may require, and safe from decay, so long as that will retains its energy. . . . Other governments are convulsed by the innovations and reforms of neighboring states; our Constitution, fixed in the affections of the people, from whose choice it has sprung, neutralizes the influence of foreign principles, and fearlessly opens an asylum to the virtuous, the unfortunate, and the oppressed of every nation."

The passage is typical, both as to style and as to doctrine. Its sincerity is so manifest that it is impossible not to admire and be touched by its ardent Americanism, its faith in popular government, in the American Constitution, and in the boundless success of the United States through material progress and the simple arts of peace. But a generation which has grown accustomed to less use of literary as well as other stimulants

probably finds its eloquence somewhat tur-
gid, and tempers its enthusiasm with the
sadder consciousness of a success less perfect
than was anticipated. The same qualities
and the same defects are to be found in all
the subsequent volumes of the work ; up to
its completion in 1885, it still continued, as
our phrase is, to vote for Jackson. But if
there had been, meantime, no change in the
fundamental principles, there was a great
improvement in the workmanship. It is
sufficient evidence of this to point to the
rate of production of the individual volumes.
The first three volumes appeared in 1834,
1837, and 1840; the next three, after a
period of political and diplomatic life, in
1852, 1853, and 1854 ; the seventh and
eighth, at intervals a little greater; the ninth,
not until 1866 ; the tenth, in 1874 ; the two
concluding volumes, as late as 1882.

From 1846 to 1849, the historian was our
minister to England, and from 1866 to 1874
he was minister in Germany. The result
was the collection of an enormous mass of
material from the archives of foreign states,
and from the stores of family correspondence. Because of the long duration and
the great fame of his researches, similar

opportunities, almost unlimited in extent, were at his service in this country. Sometimes his narrative seems too much dominated by the possession of the abundant materials of this class to which his prefaces refer with so conscious a pride. The last volumes are limited in scope, giving a history of little but military and diplomatic movements during the Revolution. Perhaps it is as well. Bancroft's talents for the narration of military and diplomatic history were of a very high order. He had great skill in marshalling large arrays of facts, good judgment, and a lucid and picturesque style. On the other hand, a history of popular movements, of public opinion and of the internal development of the United States, would exhibit at the greatest disadvantage the author's faults, — not only his loud and uncritical Americanism and his rhetorical bias, but the superficiality of his insight into national psychology, his failure to perceive its complexities, his tendency to conventionalize, to compose his American populations of highly virtuous Noah's-ark men. The excursuses in which he attempts this are among the least happy and adequate portions of his work.

An interesting though far from pleasing episode in the history of Bancroft's labors was the chapter of controversies with critics. A slighting remark respecting a predecessor, in the second volume of the history, had drawn upon the historian the wrath of the old president of Harvard College, who soon showed that his Federalist pen had not lost its incisiveness and vigor. For reasons partly personal, partly political, Bancroft was highly unpopular in the literary society of Boston, and not a few attacks followed. The ninth volume of the history, dealing with a great part of the military history of the Revolution, aroused an especially large number of assailants. Descendants of Greene, Reed, Schuyler, and Sullivan, in able pamphlets, attempted to show that the historian had dealt unjustly with their respective ancestors. The historian was so much superior to his critics in knowledge and skill, that in most cases he seemed to come off victorious from the encounter. But the careful reader of this mass of controversial literature will probably feel that a good number of the criticisms made were just, especially as concerned Bancroft's use of quotations, which he sometimes so excises and transposes as

10

strangely to pervert their meaning. He will note, too, the haughtiness and acerbity of temper with which criticisms were received, the slender recognition of fellow-laborers, and, where criticisms had been supported by proof, the grudging and minimized acknowledgment of error. But, in spite of all these defects, the American people owe a great debt to the famous historian who has just departed, after a long lifetime spent in enthusiastic study and inspiring exposition of their history.

A few words should be said concerning some other writers of the period, who gave themselves to the sober field of American history. It would be pleasant to be able to say more than a word of Peter Force, of whose great collection of the " American Archives " Congress published nine volumes and then stopped. To the lasting disgrace of Congress, all subsequent efforts have failed to obtain appropriations for the completion of this monumental work. The work of collection and publication was carried on in more varied ways by President Sparks. In making his large collections in America and Europe, and in editing the " Library of American Biography," the writings of Washington and

Franklin, and the "Diplomatic Correspondence of the Revolution," he performed services of inestimable value to American history. That he at the same time did it no
small disservice by his mode of editing, as
when he toned down the actual words of
Washington into tame correctness, was
vigorously charged by Lord Mahon and
others. Sparks's letters in answer to Mahon were models of dignified reply to
criticism. The view of the controversy
which would now be taken is, probably, that
President Sparks did not conform to all
the best rules of editing as they were then
known. It is quite true that he ought not
to be judged by the more exacting standards
of the present day; yet 1833, when Ranke
was already teaching and writing, and the
"Monumenta" had begun to be published,
was by no means in the dark ages of historical method. But there was much exaggera-
tion in the fault found with Sparks, and due
recognition of his invaluable pioneer work
will prevent extreme censoriousness as to
defects of workmanship. Gentle Washington Irving thus alludes to the fault, when
speaking of these letters in the preface of
his "Life of Washington:" —

" A careful collation of many of them
with the originals [Sparks had to work from
the letter-books mostly] convinced me of the
general correctness of the collection, . . .
and I am happy to bear this testimony to
the essential accuracy of one whom I con-
sider among the greatest benefactors to our
national literature."

Downright Hildreth alluded to it in terms
more direct.

Hildreth's own work came later, — late
enough to feel the force of increasing sec-
tional animosities, and to show the effects of
them in an unfortunate degree. A man of
very decided convictions, and ardently interested in politics, the Whig editor wrote
the " History of the United States " with a
strong partisan bias. In the first three volumes, bringing the story down to the close
of the Revolution, this naturally finds less
place, and the lucidity, directness, and accuracy of the writer made his book one of much
value, though a little dry to the general
reader. But in the last three volumes, treating the history of our national politics down
to 1821, its partisanship of the Federalists
is so manifest that all its lucidity, directness,
and general accuracy cannot wholly redeem

it. If for Federalists we substitute Demo-
crats, we shall have to say much the same
things of the otherwise excellent "History
of the United States" to 1841, which
George Tucker of Virginia published just
before the outbreak of the Civil War. In
1859 and 1860 appeared the first two volumes of the "History of New England" by
John Gorham Palfrey, as good a piece of
work as had ever been done among us; but
it belongs quite as much to the next period,
in which the remaining volumes were published; and it is time to turn to the writers
of what I have called another school.

It was something more than a difference
of subject that separated the writers already
characterized from Prescott and Motley. A
difference of attitude underlay the difference
in choice of subject. The impulses which ac-
tuated the former were founded, sometimes
in political but at any rate in national feelings. Those of the latter were rather those
of the literary man. It was only after long
hesitation and with some regret that Prescott abandoned the plan of devoting himself
entirely to the history of literature. He
was averse to politics, though the historians
of Europe have seldom been more engaged

in them than they were in his time. His
correspondence and his prefaces show us
how much the literary aspect of his work
occupied him; truthful and artistic narration
was his main aim. Writers of such predilections as these would be likely to turn away
from the sober history of their own country,
and seek their themes in the more picturesque fields of European history. The choice
of subjects which Prescott made gives the
plainest evidence of such purposes. Even
apart from the brilliant treatment which
his genius gave them, and from which it is
hard for our minds now to separate them, it
is plain that the reign of Ferdinand and
Isabella, the conquest of Mexico, the conquest of Peru, the history of Philip the
Second, were subjects eminently capable of
picturesque treatment.

The reader's interest in the volumes written upon these engaging themes is heightened by the knowledge of the difficulties
surmounted in their preparation. Like
three other eminent historians, his contemporaries, Augustin Thierry, Karl Szayno-
cha, and the Marquis Gino Capponi, he was
blind, or nearly so. Everett, speaking at
the memorial meeting of the Massachusetts

Historical Society just after his death, beau-
tifully applied to him the words of the Greek
poet, " Greatly the Muse loved him, and she
gave him both good and evil; she deprived
him of his eyes, but gave him the gift of
sweet song." Only during the composition
of the second of his books, " The Conquest
of Mexico," was he able to make any considerable use of his eyes. During a part of the
ten years given to the preparation of the
" History of Ferdinand and Isabella," and
of the time spent on the " Conquest of Peru,"
he could use them for an hour or two each
day. During the rest of the time, including
the whole period given to the " History of
Philip the Second," he was forced to rely
entirely upon the eyes of others. In fact,
his investigations for the first of his books
began by going through seven quarto volumes in Spanish, with a reader who understood not a word of the language. Better assistance was eventually procured, and
great amounts of reading were done. The
writing machine now preserved in the cabi-
net of the Massachusetts Historical Society was obtained, and released the patient
scholar from the necessity of constant dic-
tation. Fortunately, he possessed ample

means for the purchase of books. The consultation of foreign archives in person was, indeed, impracticable. But, through the kindness and exertions of devoted friends, of whom his amiable and winning character had attracted a large number, this obstacle was in a great degree removed, and the successive narratives rest on an increasing amplitude of original and unpublished documents, drawn not only from public and private repositories in Spain, but in the case of Philip the Second from most of the great collections of Western Europe. But, for all this, the writing of these eleven volumes under such disabilities remains a most remarkable achievement, and one which bears strong testimony to the high qualities of Prescott's character.

The books themselves need no factitious interest arising from the knowledge of the circumstances of their production. They are too admirable and too familiar to need praise in respect to interest of narrative, grace of style, or artistic skill in the management and marshaling of the various parts. The unity of design and beauty of detail, the romantic charm and picturesqueness which the author sought, he certainly obtained. Scarcely less

praise must be given to the conscientiousness
of his research, though it may be doubted
whether his critical insight was of the most
penetrating sort.   Nor was he a profoundly
philosophical historian, distinguished for
searching analysis.   In one of his early
private memoranda, he confesses that he
hates "hunting up latent, barren antiquities,"
and though he later, to some extent, con-
quered this repugnance, the studies which
make the analytical and sociological historian
were never thoroughly congenial to him.   It
is mainly the concrete aspects of life that
engage his interest, and as a historical painter
of these, he was, in the period of the publication of his works, the years from 1837 to
1858, without a rival, save Macaulay and
Michelet.

In the preface to the first volume of his
"Philip the Second," confessing the difficulty of imparting unity of interest to a
narrative which must necessarily embrace
topics so various, Prescott had alluded par-
ticularly to the subject of the revolt of the
Netherlands.   He had said that, though but
an episode to his own subject, this alone
might well form the theme of a separate and
extensive work, and had announced that

before long such a work might be " expected," to use his own words, " from the
pen of our accomplished countryman, Mr. J.
Lothrop Motley, who, during the last few
years, for the better prosecution of his labors,
has established his residence in the neighbor-
hood of the scenes of his narrative." The
work thus announced, the famous " Rise of
the Dutch Republic," was published in 1856.
Accordingly when, in 1859, Prescott died,
leaving his " History of Philip the Second "
no farther advanced than to the year 1580,
the historian who should in a sense continue
his work was already in the field. The first
of Motley's works carried down to the year
1584 a narrative whose subject, though not
the same as that of Prescott's last work,
necessarily had much in common with it.
For the history of the Dutch revolt against
Philip could hardly be written without saying much concerning other aspects or portions of his reign. In the year 1860 appeared the first two, in 1868 the last two,
volumes of the " History of the United
Netherlands," embracing the years 1584 to
1609. " The Life and Death of John of
Barneveld," a work in form biographical,
but really continuing the " History of the

Netherlands" for a decade more, appeared
in 1874.

Enormous labors in the investigation of
archives were performed in the preparation
of these books. Motley had the intense zeal
of the born investigator, a rare and heroic
quality of which the world takes little note
in historians. He had likewise in full possession those qualities which engage the
reader. No American has ever written a
history more brilliant and dramatic. The
subject was a noble one. It was full of
picturesque incident, of opportunities for
glowing description, of thrilling tales of
heroism. But it was not simply these that
so engaged Motley's interest that, as he
afterwards said, he felt as if he *must* write
upon it. It was a great national conflict for
freedom, and as such was profoundly congenial to one who, above all things, loved
liberty. The warm heart and enthusiastic,
ardent temper of the historian laid him open
to dangers of partiality which, it must be
confessed, he was far from wholly escaping.
The American public little appreciate the
extent to which he was influenced by such
feelings. Guizot, in a review article, noted
Motley's advocacy, but thought it too appa-

rent to do harm, and excused it as being on the right side, that of political and religious liberty. Throughout the volumes on the " Rise of the Dutch Republic," Motley is a thorough partisan of William the Silent, — a sincere and conscientious partisan, to be sure, but a partisan none the less. Some may think that it is little harm to exaggerate the virtues of William the Silent, or to soften the defects of a character so heroic ; but certainly it is a pity to add one more to the long chain of English writers who, out of ancestral prejudice, have dealt hard measure to all Spaniards. Similarly, in his narrative of the great internal contest between the adherents of Prince Maurice and the adherents of Oldenbarneveld, the Calvinists and the Arminians, it must be declared deliberately that Motley is a partisan of the latter, and is distinctly unfair to the former. It is easy to see the reasons in both cases. As a lover of liberty, the cause of William and the Netherlanders, fighting for freedom, engaged his warm affection. In the later period, his Unitarian sympathies made it natural for him to embrace the cause of the Arminians against the Calvinists. Dr. Holmes, to be sure, in his memoir of Motley,

defends him from this latter charge. The
Dutch historian, Groen van Prinsterer, in
his " Maurice et Barneveld," though express-
ing a warm admiration for Motley, has criti-
cised him as unfair to the Remonstrant
cause. With his usual keen scent for Cal-
vinism, the doctor endeavors to show that
Mr. Groen van Prinsterer has taken up this
position because he is himself a Calvinist.
But Mr. Groen van Prinsterer does not
stand alone. It should not be forgotten that,
if none of the Dutch historical writers were
as brilliant as Motley, the nation stood, in
historical scholarship, hardly second to any
in Europe; five historians could be named
every one of whom was probably as learned
in the facts as Motley himself. The dispute
is, in the end, one for the Dutch to settle,
and Dutch opinion is still divided. But so
long as the leading opinions are in general
more moderate than Motley's, and so long
as the Dutch are not " vehemently suspected "
of having more of the ardent temper of the
advocate than Motley had, we may feel justi-
fied in mingling a certain sense of partiality
with our strong admiration of his warmth,
his brilliancy, and his dramatic force.

11

IV.

THE PERIOD SINCE 1861.

WE were able to make a sharp division between the first period in the history of American historical writing and the second; the first chapter including writers who were themselves of the emigrating generation, while in the second none were included who were separated from the original settlers by a less interval than two generations. Similarly, the second period was plainly separated from the third by the revolutionary war, during the distresses and troubles of which there was little leisure for historical or other composition. The historical literature of the colonial period was confined to a few sporadic writers, not organically connected one with another; it had not acquired momentum enough to carry it in continuous life across that time of difficulty and preoccupying care.

But with the third and fourth periods the case is different. American historical liter-

ature had now acquired vitality, and hence-
forth its development was uninterrupted. If,
therefore, we select any chronological point
at which to divide this last and most important period, the point chosen will necessarily
seem from some points of view an arbitrary
one. It is quite true that the civil war
formed the starting point for many new
tendencies in our historical, as in our general literature. But, on the other hand,
much went on as before. In the first place,
some of the histories spoken of in the last
paper, though begun before the war, were
not completed until after it. The first two
volumes of Motley's " History of the United
Netherlands " had appeared in 1860; the
last two were published in 1868; and his
" Barneveld," which is virtually a continuation of them, in 1874. Another work, whose
publication similarly overlapped the fourth
period, was Palfrey's " History of New England," probably the best single large piece
of work that has been done in America on
any part of our colonial period. After much
labor in America and considerable research
in England, the first and second volumes had
been successively published just before the
war broke out. The third did not follow

until 1865 ; the fourth, not until 1875. At
the writer's death the history of the New
England colonies had been brought down to
the year 1740 ; the fifth volume, recently
published, carries it to the outbreak of the
Revolution. If Dr. Palfrey was not a man
of great insight into popular movements, and
was too constant an apologist of the rulers of
New England, his book was nevertheless
admirable on account of his extensive knowledge of sources, his industry, clearness, accuracy, and skill in narration. Among its
many excellences, one which deserves particular notice is the degree of attention which
it bestows upon the history of England itself
during the Puritan era, and upon the mutual
influence of Old England and New England
during that period of exceptionally close
sympathy and connection. Often the genius
of a writer is quite as much displayed by
new apportionments of their relative amounts
of attention to the different aspects of his
subject as in any other way, for thus his
insight into the proportions and relations of
various factors is practically displayed.

Meanwhile, other historians, not in the
field during the preceding period, have continued the traditions of the school which has

been described in a previous article under the names of Prescott and Motley. An especially close example of this is the case of John Foster Kirk, who was one of the private secretaries successively employed by Prescott, and who, after Prescott's death, wrote a valuable book upon the " History of Charles the Bold," a contribution in the same general field as that of his master's labors. But the author who has most conspicuously continued the school of picturesque historians is Francis Parkman, the eminent historian of the French dominion in North America.

The subject is one highly attractive to an American historical writer of this school, who wishes at the same time that his studies shall not be too remote from his own age and country. Chivalry and heroism and romantic adventure, the glamour of a foreign civilization and the poetic charm of unfamiliar forms of religion, are all there ; but the story has also a close and important relation with the growth of our own nation. Prescott had been able to impart an additional interest to his " History of Ferdinand and Isabella " because of the episode formed by the voyages of Columbus ; and perhaps Mot-

ley's history of the struggle of the Dutch
for independence may have had a special
interest for the general reader in a country
of whose history a struggle for independence
is one of the most familiar portions.   Prescott, too, had chosen distinctly American
subjects in his " Conquest of Mexico " and
his " Conquest of Peru."   But no one of
these had so direct a bearing on our national
history as the story of New France.   For
several generations some of the most important English colonies were occasionally men-
aced and always limited by the presence
upon their frontier of a considerable military
power established there by a nation usually
unfriendly.   Furthermore, the presence of
this power was one of the chief influences
toward colonial consolidation, and its final
removal was one of the causes which made
possible the revolt from the government of
Great Britain.   It is therefore with good
reason that the general title given to the
whole series of Mr. Parkman's narratives is,
" France and England in North America."

The project of a series·of so wide a scope
developed gradually in the writer's mind.
Soon after graduation from college he had
gone on several occasions to make more or

less extensive visits to the wild regions of
the Northwest. Much of his subsequent
historical work shows the effects of the familiarity thus gained with the scenery and
men of the wilderness. One of these effects
was the choice, for the subject of his first
historical production, of the Conspiracy of
Pontiac. It was from this work that the
writer was led on to the preparation of a
series of historical narratives upon the whole
course of the French dominion in America,
its relations to the English colonies, and its
final destruction by the military power of
Great Britain. For the history of Pontiac's
conspiracy forms a natural sequel to the
history of the French and Indian war, and
to that of New France generally.

This book completed, therefore, and published in 1851, the author went back to take
up at the beginning the history of the French
in North America, the great task upon which
he has been engaged ever since, and which
is now nearly completed. As in the case of
Prescott, physical difficulties which might
well seem insurmountable opposed. Extreme
ill health made it always necessary to con-
fine mental exertion within narrow limits,
and more than once stopped it entirely for

several years at a time. Weakness of sight
seems to have made it always impossible to
read or write continuously for much more
than five minutes, while once, at least, it has
been for a period of three years impossible
to endure the light of day, or to read or
write to the smallest extent.

But the volumes composed under the pressure of these calamities need no indulgence
from the critic. It may almost be said that
they need no praise, so widely spread and so
permanent has been their fame. The first
of the series, though published only twenty-
seven years ago, has already long passed its
twentieth edition. Others are approaching
it. The series has shown a continuous improvement, and especially in thoroughness
and fullness of research. It is in this respect,
indeed, that American historians have, at
the outset of their careers, been least adequately provided. In Germany the class of
historical writers and the class of historical
professors are so nearly identical that the
young student who starts out upon a career
of historical authorship has almost always
the advantage of having learned his trade
under a teacher experienced in it. In other
words, with all the opportunity it presents,

and the need it has for that genius and insight and maturity which can neither be
communicated nor described, there are many
things in the more technical portions of the
pursuit which by long experience have been
reduced to practical rules ; and these rules
can be learned of a master, if only by imita-
tion. But English and American historical
writers have till lately worked so much in
isolation that they could have no apprenticeship in the communicable portions of the
art. In the highly developed arts of research and of historical criticism, therefore,
our historians have started out uninstructed,
and have learned these as they went on, with
no other teachers than their own mistakes
and their constant desire for completeness.
There has also been a great improvement in
the always brilliant and engaging style of
Mr. Parkman, which, with increasing years,
has grown more severe in taste.

The first book of the projected series was
called " Pioneers of France in the New
World." Its first part described in fascina-
ting narrative the history of the Huguenot
settlement in Florida, and its extinction by
the Spanish ; the second took up the story
of the permanent beginnings of the French

dominion, the settlement of Acadia, and the labors of Champlain and his associates. The next volume, published two years later, continues the story from 1635 to 1652, under the title of " The Jesuits in North America." For this volume especially, the author was able to make great use of his early acquired knowledge of Indian character and civilization ; the sublime devotion of the missionaries and their heroic endurance of torture and martyrdom at the hands of the savages confer upon it an additional and most touching interest. The next volume, " La Salle and the Discovery of the Great West," treats of an episode, though an episode whose consequences were at one time likely to be highly important. The volume called " The Old Régime in Canada " is devoted, after the narration of the history of the transitional period 1652–1672, to a description of Canadian government and life, in chapters carefully based on original sources, and of surpassing interest. The ablest of the colonial governors and the history down to 1701 are treated in the volume called " Count Frontenac and New France under Louis XIV." The intermediate period to 1748 having been left for the time being, Mr.

Parkman has given us the conclusion in "Montcalm and Wolfe," two volumes, the best in the series, on that American portion of the seven years' war which we are wont to call the French and Indian war.

It will be seen how wide is the range of interest covered by these volumes. They are not simply a history of a great attempt to create, under the forms of absolute monarchy, feudalism, and Catholicism, a centralized and military power. Nor are they simply a history of the efforts of that power to overbalance and check the system of free, Protestant and English colonies, unorganized and discordant indeed, but strong with the strength of popular institutions, of love of freedom, and of habits of individual initiative. This alone would be sufficient to make the tale bright and commanding. But we have also the adventures of explorers and traders, the achievements of missionaries, the heroism of martyrs, the wild life of the Indian tribes, the scenery of the forest, the events of war, the brilliant picture of French aristocracy transferred, for purposes of war or government or devotion, to the wilds of America; and it cannot be said that the writer has proved unequal to the adequate treatment of a single one of these so varied elements of interest.

I have devoted much space to Mr. Parkman as being, next after one or two who survived from the preceding period, the most conspicuous figure in the American historiography of the last twenty-five years, the only historian who can fairly be called classical. No one can predict the advent of genius, but it appears not very likely that the roll of the classical historians will be much increased in the immediate future, or that the next generation will in this respect abound in eminent names.   Amiel says : —

" The era of mediocrity in all things is commencing.   Equality begets uniformity, and we divest ourselves of the bad by sacrificing the eminent, the remarkable, the extraordinary."

Such, at any rate, is likely to be the case with our historical writing for a long time. Nor is it in the main to be regretted.   If there is not produced among us any work of supereminent genius, there will surely be a large amount of good second-class work done ; that is, of work of the second class in respect to purely literary qualities.   Now it is the spread of thoroughly good second-class work

— second-class in this sense — that our science most needs at present; for it sorely needs that improvement in technical process, that superior finish of workmanship, which a large number of works of talent can do more to foster than a few works of literary genius. If, therefore, that leveled Americanism toward which M. Renan tells us that the world is now progressing is, in the matter of historical work, to take among us the form which we have been supposing, we need not lament. We may even hope that out of improved scholarship may grow in time a superior profundity of thought; for in truth profundity of thought has not been among the merits of any of our most distinguished historians. We may do well to remember that, in the historical literature of Europe, when the Anakim of the sixteenth century were replaced by the mousing but erudite Bollandists and Benedictines of the seventeenth and the first half of the eighteenth, it was only that the way might be prepared, by patient and scholarly accumulation of materials, for the advent of a school of historians more philosophical and profound than any that had preceded.

But the series of American historians to

which Motley and Parkman belong was not characterized solely by the pursuit, in general, of literary ends. Another distinguishing mark was its devotion to European rather than to American history. In our time the devotees of European history are not numerous in the United States (indeed, if one can judge from the contents of our magazines, European history is hardly at all a matter of interest to most Americans); and such devotees as there are have not all inherited the literary traditions. A few scholars have done excellent work in church history, for the cultivation of which a special society has been formed. Most eminent among these is the learned layman whose "History of the Inquisition" has reflected so much honor upon American scholarship. Almost no American has done anything worth while in the study of ancient history. This is a striking fact, when one thinks of it. The history of Rome, especially, offers, one would think, much that should interest Americans. There is even a similarity of national. character; the faces upon Roman busts are such as one might see any day in the streets of New York or Philadelphia. When one considers how large a place the study of the classics

has long had in American education, one
cannot help feeling that such lack of interest
in the history of the classical nations indicates that the instruction has not been sufficiently vital. On the other hand, a very
respectable number of scholars are at work
in lines of Oriental history.

Of those who have occupied themselves
with modern history, some indeed have written with a view mainly to the construction
of a picturesque narrative; but mixed with
these there has been an increasing number
of workers whose aims have been chiefly
scientific. An accomplished teacher, with a
few advanced students, has published essays
upon Anglo-Saxon law. Several Boston law-
yers have published important studies in the
history of English law. Here a historical
scholar devotes himself to the study of the
merchant-guild, or meditates the vexed subject of early landholding among the Ger-
mans; there another illustrates the history
of the Prussian state. Another labors upon
the history of sacerdotal celibacy, benefit of
clergy, ordeal, and wager of battle. All this
would have seemed very dry to the last generation; but the most judicious of the moderns see in it a hopeful sign for the future

of the science, a sign that what work is done among us in European history hereafter will be, in increasing proportion, solid in construction and addressed not unsuccessfully to superior and specialized intelligence.

We have been speaking of departments of historical work in America upon which the war had little effect, and in whose development it could only arbitrarily be taken as a dividing point. But with work upon our own history, which has occupied an increasing proportion of our attention, it is otherwise. Its character has been profoundly affected by that great conflict. Not that we have yet had the best that we shall have in the way of books on the conflict itself. We have had excellent pieces of military history, a host of regimental histories and war articles. But the books which have attempted to deal with its political aspects have been, with a few exceptions like that of Mr. Alexander Stephens, hopelessly unfair, full of crude assumption, impervious to argument. The remedy for all these things will be the coming forward of the younger generation, whose motive for studying the war is not that of personal participation.

But the mental effects·have extended far

more widely than this, far more widely than
the whole field of history, in fact. The literature, the art indeed, of the United States
can never again be like what it was before
the civil war. It was not simply that the
government became more firmly consoli-
dated, the people more closely bound together. The nation emerged from that terrible struggle adult and mature. It was
able to look upon itself and the world around
it, its past and its future, at once with more
sobriety and discrimination, and with a
heightened self-respect, born of the sense
that great achievements and sacrifices for
inspiring causes had vindicated to it a right
to independent views. Colonial attitudes of
thought ceased, as colonial attitudes in politics had ceased after the war of 1812. National sensitiveness to condescending criticism from Europeans lost its acuteness; we
began to feel, not in vanity, but in sobriety,
that now we were as worthy as they. We
began to look at our characteristics and
modes of life with an externality of view
unknown to the preceding generation. It
was possible for the international novelist to
arise, — that is, the novelist, to whom the
American is not undoubtedly the greatest of

all human types, but simply one human type among several, all alike to be exhibited with intelligent candor. Mr. Howells's voice, speaking to the American of forty years ago, would have been the voice of one crying in the wilderness, — a wilderness of vociferous panegyric upon all things American, whose very vociferousness betrayed a latent uneasiness. The development of our architecture, the gradual abandonment of Gothic and Renaissance styles for earlier styles, plainer, more Roman, more suited to the genius of a practical people, is another illustration. For the first time in our history we have become a self-reliant nation.

In the domain of American history, the change has taken effect in two directions or modes. In the first place, we have become more critical and discriminating, have learned more nearly to look upon the course of American history with an impartial eye, from the standpoint of an outsider. In the second place, there has ensued a broadening of the field of investigation and work, that its scope may correspond to the scheme of things in America, to the configuration of actual affairs. We are no longer content to adopt the same plans of distribution of

attention to different phases of history which
has seemed proper to European historians.
Our writers recognize, consciously or unconsciously, that here the elements of life have
been mixed in different proportions, and that
history should conform to these different
proportions as equally valid and worthy of
observance.

To take at once one of the most important
illustrations of this, one of the most vital
differences between European history and
that of the United States. It seems to be a
fact that the scope of statesmanship, the
influence of great individuals upon the general life, has been far less extensive here
than there. It is certain to be so in new
countries; in them Nature is supreme. Why
was it that, while Greece itself was produ-
cing statesmen, the colonial Greeks of Sicily
produced none? Simply because the abundance of Nature left no field for them. In
modern Europe the pressure of population
upon the means of subsistence, and all the
difficulties which beset the general life wher-
ever the gifts of Nature are not superabundant for the needs of man, have raised such
problems for man to cope with, such tasks
for the forces of human intelligence, as have

necessarily evoked great administrative statesmen.

But with us it has not been so. Just as
our national housekeeping has not needed,
and therefore has not developed, the scientific financial methods of burdened Europe,
the vastness of our national resources solv-
ing of itself every problem, so in general
Nature has managed for us, and economic
and other conditions have with peculiar completeness shaped our course. The govern-
mental ideas which have been represented
by the Straffords, the Richelieus, the Tur-
gots, the Pitts, the Bismarcks of the old
world (I do not mean ideas of absolutism,
but ideas of dominant influence of great intellects upon national destinies), have been
alien to America. Once, indeed, the effort
was made to apply to America the methods
of European administrative statesmanship.
That is, if I am not mistaken, the essence
of the Federalist experiment, more deeply
its characteristic than any phase of its attitude towards the American Constitution.
And why did the Federalist experiment
break down ? Simply because of those
forces which the Hebrew war song indicates
when it declares that the stars in their

courses fought against Sisera. Nature would
rule. With the advent of Jeffersonian democracy, the reins were thrown upon her neck;
and from that time to this the field of influence of natural conditions upon our national destiny has been peculiarly great, the
field of influence of great individuals far
smaller than in the Old World. All this
imposes upon our historical scholars a duty
to which they have been far more disposed
to conform since the attainment of a firmer
national self-respect. They do not properly
reflect the life that they seek to reflect if
they write solely of individual persons or
groups of persons and their conscious efforts;
they must cease blindly to follow European
schemes, and study economic and natural
conditions and developments, the unintended
growth of institutions and modes of life, the
unconscious movements and changes of
masses of men.

That this need of emancipation from the
traditions and conventions of European historiography has been making itself felt, consciously or unconsciously, is plain to any one
who surveys the historical literature of our
day. Never was there a time in America
when so great a proportion of the best his-

torical work was devoted to the subject of
the history of institutions and economics.
One writes of the history of finance; another,
of the fortunes of institutions transplanted
westward, and the genesis of governmen-
tal ideas among the lawless frontiersmen;
another, of the history of coöperation; still
another, of movements of migratory population, and the influence of German or other
national elements absorbed into our mass.
The magazine writers give us series of articles on colonial manners and customs rather
than on colonial wars. One writer even
attempts the difficult task of writing a general history of our people. The historical
publications of our universities are mostly
devoted to the history of institutions and
economics. Forty years ago, a man might
write on the diplomacy of the American
Revolution; nowadays, he is much more
likely to write on the history of the produce
exchange, or government land-grants for
railways, or education. Monographs in the
field of sociological history or on special
topics of the history of civilization are the
characteristic feature of our present historical literature.

One field indeed, whose cultivation would

naturally go along with these, is not yet
receiving adequate attention, the study,
namely, of the thought or inner life of our
nation, of public opinion, of popular movements, political and other. It is not that we
have no one corresponding to M. Renan;
for the union of so subtle and profound an
insight, so delicate and sympathetic an ap-
preciation, and so exquisite a style, is not to
be expected in a raw and youthful nation,
and indeed has scarcely appeared before in
any nation. But it is a matter of surprise
that, with the exception of a few such books
as Mr. Royce's " California," there seems
but little tendency to the cultivation of that
branch of history which may best be described as the study of the development of
national psychology. But perhaps this will
come in time.

This has been spoken of as the most important tendency of the historical writing of
America to-day, not because its votaries or
its productions are numerically in a majority,
for that may very likely not be the case, but
because of the belief that it is intrinsically
the strongest tendency, and has the future
with it. It is dangerous to prophesy; but
there are good reasons why such a prophecy

may not be too audacious. The history of
every science is in some degree conditioned
by the natural course of things in the world
at large; but it appears true, and will perhaps even have been shown by these papers,
that this is in a peculiar degree the case
with the science of history. Views of the
past, and ways of looking at it, change with
the changing complexion of the present.
But it is always found that the actual march
of affairs is far in advance of its expression
in literary theory and literary practice.
Democracy had for some time been established among us before the poetry of democracy arose. The world changes, but our
view of it does not change so fast; only with
great effort can it be kept up to date, so to
speak. Accordingly, it may be possible to
discern in the face of things at present
something which may be relied on to shape
in part the historical science of the immediate future. Those characteristics of American existence which have been mentioned
seem deeply rooted, permanent, essential;
therefore it is likely that the adjustment of
the sphere of our historical writing into con-
formity with the actual facts, relations, and
proportions of our national existence will go

on to still further completeness, and that
this tendency affords some presage as to its
predominant qualities in the immediate future, — qualities catholic and philosophical,
and contributory rather to historical science
than to historical literature.

Of course not everything is sharing, or is
likely to share, in this onward current. In
particular, the tendencies of many of our
numerous local historical societies form a
counter-current, or, better, an eddy, in which
chips of ancient timber float placidly round
and round in the same little circle, quite
unaffected by any general currents whatever.
Most of them are very useful, and those of
the West, at any rate, seem to be exceedingly active. But, with a few bright exceptions, our older historical societies seem a
little inaccessible to new ideas, and more
than a little wedded to tradition. The
thought of touching anything that occurred
since the Revolution, that is, of having anything to do with the most important part of
our history, seems seldom to occur to them.
Indeed, it is good fortune if the really active
members are not absorbed exclusively in the
study of the early voyages and discoveries,
or of the Indians, the two subjects most re-

mote from the present affairs of the United States, and therefore great favorites.

It is not likely that the more popular sort of books will change greatly in any short time. The voluminous and copiously illustrated county and city histories, with which swift and enterprising compilers from time to time present us, will probably not be much affected. Provided adequate attention has been given to the essential parts of their work, the advertisements of important industries and the engravings of prominent citizens, it will not be worth while to alter a method which has hitherto served well enough the main purpose of such publications. Indeed, it is to be expected that a large number of even the books of leading importance, whose ideas gradually filter into the popular books and school text-books, will continue to be constructed in accordance with the plans traditional to the art. This, provided it is not done from mere blindness or imperviousness to new ideas, will not be regretted. No one quarrels with Mr. Henry Adams for confining his brilliant and instructive books mainly to the political and constitutional history of the periods which they treat, or with Mr. Schouler for a similar

course. There is still a vast work remaining
to be done in our political history pure and
simple. The main object is not the cessation
of all former varieties of work, but the addition of numberless new ones, and the per-
vasion of all with more modern and catholic
ideas.

But now as to the channels through which
the historical movement of the present time
goes on, and those likely to be used in the
immediate future. With but a few exceptions, the local historical societies are not
likely to be of great use in this way. Historical scholars of a modern spirit are no
longer much in the habit of using their
transactions as media of communication with
the world. The newly founded American
Historical Association, on the other hand,
may be put to very good uses. The founding of that society was a most hopeful sign.
If adequately supported by the real workers,
it may prove of signal benefit to the progress
of the science in the future. The scope of
its publications is broad and national. Its
connections with the government will enable
it to publish still more, and out of it may
grow a Historical Manuscripts Commission,
which would be likely to accomplish as much

for history among us as the prototype has
accomplished in England. Whether through
this channel or not, the government will not
probably much longer delay to engage in
some scheme of historical publication. Several state governments are now carrying out
such enterprises.

Of our few historical magazines, most are
the organs of one or another of the local
societies; and of the more general ones it
is hard to speak with much patience. The
fault lies mostly with the general public, who
have not yet begun to care much for good
historical work. Indeed, for any essay in the
domain of European history it is scarcely
possible to think of any American outlet, now
that our old-fashioned reviews have become
extinct or worse. As for American history,
what appears in the historical magazines is
mostly of a very popular sort; it is only on
condition of their maintaining such a composition that the " intelligent public " allows
them to continue to exist at all. Meanwhile,
however, the great literary magazines have
opened their columns to series of good popular articles upon colonial or revolutionary
history, or even the general or the more
recent history of the United States, the last

and apparently the most successful of such ventures being the war articles of "The Century" magazine. Very likely this indicates, or may succeed in creating, a more general interest in history among the unprofessional. Meanwhile, the scientific workers may find an avenue of publication through the hospitable columns of the new "English Historical Review," since the prospect of having one of their own is exceedingly remote.

A method of historical publication much in vogue among us at present is that of putting forth a series of volumes by separate authors upon kindred subjects. We have had a series of "Campaigns of the Civil War," a series of "Lesser Wars of the United States," with some others, and, perhaps more conspicuous to the public eye, the "American Statesmen" series and the series on "American Commonwealths." The plan has its advantages and its defects. From the point of view of the publisher, it is eminently well-conceived. Greater attention is drawn to individual pieces of work when thus collected; greater interest is excited in the general subject when a mass of work upon it is presented. To some extent, the interests of the publishing business and of

historical scholarship are identical. Whatever increases the audience and the influence of good work must be welcomed by the
scholar. But it must not be forgotten — and
some of the volumes on "American Statesmen" and "American Commonwealths" are
illustrations of the fact — that, in a series
of this sort, the good books bolster up the
poor ones, and gain them a factitious repute
and power. At the same time, the best
books suffer from the general average, seldom acquiring more weight than their frac-
tion of the collective weight of the series, nor
as much as might accrue to them as independent publications. Another result is,
that all the kindred subjects therein com-
prised, however various in many characteristics, are bound down to the same uniform
fullness and style of treatment. If Alexander Hamilton is to have a volume of three
hundred pages sextodecimo, so must Gou-
verneur Morris. Statesman A, whose life
was spent in executive affairs, may be treated
differently from Statesman B, who spent his
life on the bench, but he will not be treated
with anything like so strong a difference as
the facts demand. If, as Mr. Bagehot says,
" the genius of great affairs abhors nicety of

division," still more does it abhor equality of
division; and their treatment should correspond to their genius.

It is well worth while to take such consid-
erations into account in any survey of our
present state and prospects, because a tendency to more organization of historical
work is just now very marked. It is not
simply a result of that progression towards
equality, that fading of individual saliency,
which we have before noted. It is a tendency peculiarly American. A nation singularly devoted to business has transferred
to the fields of literature and science the
habits of business management. We edu-
cate by correspondence, we facilitate literary
work by ingenious mechanical devices, we
catalogue and systematize. No nation in
the world is so addicted to bibliography and
indexing. The English still, as frequently
as not, publish books without indexes; the
American who does such a thing is at once
denounced by our reviewers as ripe for any
atrocity. To say nothing of smaller bibliog-
raphies, Sabin's great dictionary of "Americana" already extends to about twoscore
volumes, and will, when completed, embrace
as many as a hundred thousand titles.

But we are going further in the organization of historical work, even to the writing of histories by organized forces, or by coöperation. An excellent instance is the preparation of a most extensive history of the Pacific Coast by the staff of trained assistants employed by a wealthy, able, and enthusiastic Californian historian, Mr. H. H. Bancroft. Retiring from the publishing business with great wealth, Mr. Bancroft has employed the energy and the methods of a business man in the collection, digestion, and presentation of materials. First, a great library has been collected, including all obtainable books bearing at all upon the history of Central America, Mexico, California, Utah, Oregon, British Columbia, and Alaska. Thousands of Mexican and Californian pamphlets have been gathered, and files of hundreds of newspapers from all parts of the Pacific Coast. Numerous valuable manuscripts have fallen into the collector's hands, and enormous masses of manuscript copies of state records and mission archives have been made specially for the library by his secretaries. Old pioneers still surviving have been visited, and their recollections taken down at great length. A Russian assistant was sent to Alaska to copy the government records there. Half a dozen Spanish ones have done similar work. From twelve to twenty accomplished linguists, we are told, have been constantly employed in Mr. Bancroft's service since 1869. Secretaries have all this time been reading, translating, summarizing, cataloguing, and indexing the whole collection.

The result, attained at the cost of half a million dollars, is a mass of systematized information, such as must make the users and the desirers of historical materials elsewhere deeply envious, and for the collection of which, under ordinary methods, even an antediluvian lifetime would scarcely suffice a historian. The highest praise must be given to the zeal for research, the public spirit, and the enterprise and care which have presided over the formation of this priceless collection. But when it comes to writing history by this same method, some reserves are necessarily suggested to the mind. Mr. Bancroft has prepared from these materials, and published, a gigantic " History of the Pacific States of America," in thirty-four unusually large volumes. It is obvious that a work of such magnitude, carried through in so few years, could not possibly be written by a single hand. In fact, the books were first written by the various members of the cohort of assistants, and the person whose name they bear has simply revised, as a sort of managing editor, the productions of this highly-organized staff. Valuable as the work proves to be, some of the faults of such a plan are evident. There can be no fixing of responsibility. No one knows whom to criticise. No one can know whether the authority of this or that part of the book, or of the whole, should be much or little. Moreover, there is less likelihood, under such a system, of the best historical criticism, the most skillful sifting of the evidence thus elaborately collected. But all this is on the supposition that the main object of historical composition is correctness of detail, that a book is perfect if none of its information is erroneous; a supposition by no means to be admitted. To any one who has any conception of the use of the higher powers, the rarer qualities of the mind, in historical composition, it will be plain that no really great history can be written by the methods of the " literary bureau," by hiring a force of assistants and seeing that they do it. It

may almost be said that the historian, like
the poet, is born, not made; but if he is
made, he is not made by machinery.

Such dangers as have been above noted
must always, in greater or less degree, attend
work prepared by these or similar methods.
It is important to observe this, because one
sees, in this country so devoted to organization, a growing tendency toward the production of historical work in such ways, the
application to it of the economic principle
and method of division of labor. A far
greater amount of work can thus be put
forth, and, what perhaps is quite as important, can be put forth in such a way as
greatly to increase its force upon the world;
for work so combined and systematized with
other work is not in danger of being lost or
ineffectual, as are, for instance, the disser-
tations so ingeniously concealed in German
university and school programmes. But it
is well to remember that with these advantages there are some serious drawbacks.
Good work of the second class, and great
amounts of it, can thus be done; good work
of the first class cannot. The tale of Pega-
sus in harness has this meaning, that the
finest qualities of the human mind cannot

be thus systematized. The highest intellects are not at the service of the hirers of clerks, are not to be made cogs or wheels in a history-producing machine.

By far the most noteworthy of our cooperative histories is the "Narrative and Critical History of America," edited by Mr. Justin Winsor. With its chapters of historical narrative by our most learned and able historical scholars, each writing upon his own special field, and with its critical essays upon the sources of information, it seems without doubt to be the most important and useful contribution ever yet made to American historical science. It splendidly sums up the historical labors of a century. And, by the way, consisting so largely as it does of a bibliographical record of what has been done, the proportion between its parts affords a striking indication of the relative amounts of work which Americans have expended on different portions of American history. It has taken four volumes to set forth the results achieved in our colonial and revolutionary history, while a single volume is thought to suffice for the period from 1789 to 1850. Another editor might divide the work somewhat differently; but the fact remains that we have expended much more labor on the earlier than on the later period of our history. Perhaps new nations have a passion for the study of origins; or perhaps even those who write history enjoy an interesting story, and find more such in colonial history than in. later times. The disproportion indicated is a necessary incident to the scheme of the work. There are also, it should be noted, other limitations which must to some extent beset all co-operative or monographic histories alike. Stretched on the Procrustean bed of uniform requirements in respect to extensiveness and general method of treatment, the authors can present only those things which they have in common, — abundant and correct information, and acute historical criticism. Many of the finer qualities of the individual mind are likely to evaporate in the process; much of what is most valuable in individual views and conceptions of history will find no place for itself. No one who appreciates these will readily assent to the assertion, in the prospectus to the " Narrative and Critical History," that, " when the superiority of the coöperative method is fully understood, the individual historian, if he

14

ventures forth at all, will be read for enter-
tainment rather than profit."

And now as to the agents by whom historical science is to be furthered. Here,
also, the present enables us to judge somewhat of the future. It is not probable that
the advance-guard of our army will be led
by the ruling members of the various local
historical societies. Nor, on the other hand,
will much be done by the class of professionally literary men. At New York, we
are assured, there is now a literary centre,
and in and near it a literary class ; and lest
the public should lose sight of the fact, each
of our great magazines has at times an article by some one of the number in which the
rest are commemorated, each star being catalogued by these prompt astronomers as soon
as it succeeds in getting at all above the
horizon. But with these complacent Augus-
tans, literature appears to be mostly a branch
of journalism, and history has little to expect
from them. No doubt their school surpasses
in breadth and the cosmopolitan quality
that which forty years ago had its centre in
Boston, but it is as much inferior in scholarship as it is in dignity. The local antiqua-
ries, the professionally literary men, and the

men of wealth and leisure devoted to study,
will no doubt continue to write historical
books. But an increasing proportion of the
annual product now comes from the teachers
of history in universities and colleges, and
the signs are that the immediate future belongs to the professorial class.

The change is more significant than may
at first be seen. Its meaning will appear if
we bear in mind that want of early training
in the technique of historical research and
composition which has been already spoken
of as characteristic of American historians
hitherto. The increasing identification of the
writing and the teaching classes may be relied on to remove this obstacle to progress.
The next generation will have served an
apprenticeship under men who write ; and
the superior finish, the improvement in scholarly method, which have been so much
needed, will be one of the results. Already,
increasing numbers of special students of
history are frequenting those universities
which afford graduate instruction, and if the
annual production of books and other publications giving evidence of scientific training and of high ideals of historical scholarship is still small, it is visibly increasing.

Thus we have traced the development of our science from its half-conscious infancy down to the present time, and perhaps a little way into the future. It cannot truly be said that it has yet reached anything like maturity, but it is in a vigorous though raw adolescence.